LE GAVROCHE COOKBOOK
MICHEL ROUX JR

D1573291

27. September. 2000

Thank you for a glorious dinner.
We will never forget it!
with love & thanks,

[signature]

22/3/82 7.35
ALL OR NOTHING

Ringo Starr [signature]

Merci. C'est un honneur de signer votre
livre d'or.
Jean Louis Trintignant
Janvier 2000

3/12/87 Thank you for a memorable time

Diana Rigg

[signature]

[signature] Mason

Aug 15
1993
Woody
Allen *[signature]*

To La Gavroche

Thank you for the
lovely food !

[signature]

Le Gavroche Cookbook

Michel Roux jr

Photography by Jean Cazals

CASSELL&CO

Since Le Gavroche opened in 1967, many colorful and illustrious guests have signed the visitors' book. PAGE 2, CLOCKWISE FROM TOP LEFT: Gwyneth Paltrow, Ringo Starr, Diana Rigg, James Mason, Madonna, Woody Allen, Ingrid Bergman, Jean Louis Trintignant

First published in the United Kingdom in 2001 by Cassell & Co

Distributed in the United States by Sterling Publishing Co. Inc.
387 Park Avenue South, New York, N.Y. 100 16-88 10

ISBN 0 304 36190 9

Editorial director Susan Haynes
Design director David Rowley
Edited by Maggie Ramsay
Designed by Nigel Soper
Printed and bound in Italy by Printer Trento S.r.l.

Cassell & Co
Wellington House
125 Strand
London WC2R 0BB

This book is about the enjoyment of
life around a table. For me, this is
never quite fulfilled without
Emily and Gisele

CONTENTS

Introduction

When Le Gavroche opened, I was seven years old. How could I have guessed that more than thirty years later our family's restaurant would still be counted among the best in Britain— or that I would be running the show? In fact, it is now nearly ten years since I took charge of the kitchen, and naturally, from time to time, I pause to reflect on the history of the restaurant and how it has evolved over the years. This book has been taking shape in my mind for several years, and the year 2000 seemed a good time to sit down and write it, for a number of reasons. Not only would it be a way of marking the new millennium, it would also mark 33 years of Le Gavroche, a pretty unusual anniversary in this business, where the average lifespan of a restaurant is considerably less than ten years. So many restaurants, especially in our major cities, seem to explode on to the scene in a burst of public relations hype, then enjoy a period when they are in vogue and can do no wrong, only to fade away sadly before they have reached even their fifth anniversary.

Happily, Le Gavroche has never really been out of fashion, and is currently going through a halcyon period, winning award after award and receiving honorable mentions from an increasingly international media.

On a more personal note, I also wanted to show that my uncle [Michel Roux, whose autobiography *Life is a Menu* was published earlier this year] is not the only literary genius in the family—nor the only Michel Roux!

Le Gavroche remains essentially true to its roots in classic French cuisine, and the contents of this book reflect this. The recipes are those we serve in the restaurant, the only difference being in the details of the presentation; with a brigade of chefs it takes only seconds to finish a dish with a final flourish, but for the home cook I truly believe a simpler approach is more appropriate. All the recipes—bar one or two, perhaps—are relatively easy for a confident cook to prepare, as long as you have a little experience and are not afraid to get stuck in. Cooking, like anything else that is worth doing, takes time and thought. Some of the recipes in this book need to be planned well in advance of serving, but there are plenty of others that can be made quite quickly and, with a glass of wine, salad, and maybe some cheese or fruit to follow, form a simple and satisfying meal in their own right.

The recipes are arranged by season to make shopping and menu planning easier, but don't feel obliged to stick to recipes from only one season. A few ingredients, such as certain summer fruit and game in the fall, are difficult to find out of season, but if you remain on the lookout for the freshest and best ingredients I hope you will enjoy dipping into this book throughout the year.

Michel Roux

LONDON, DECEMBER 2000

Le Gavroche: the story of the restaurant

In April 1967, while London was in the midst of a cultural revolution, a little restaurant in Lower Sloane Street, not far from Kings Road, opened its doors for the first time. This was to be the beginning of the culinary revolution in London. Le Gavroche was not cheap, but it offered food that previously could be found only in France.

It was the realization of a long-held dream of the two brothers, Michel and Albert Roux. Six years apart in age, the sons and grandsons of *charcutiers*, both had followed the traditional career path of French chefs, beginning at the age of fourteen as apprentice *pâtissiers*, then moving to the kitchens of the British Embassy in Paris, famous in the 1950s for the excellence of the food served at its receptions. In 1959 Albert moved to Kent, England, to take up the position of chef to Major Peter Cazalet, racehorse trainer to, among others, the Queen Mother. Meanwhile, following his military service, in 1963 Michel became private chef to Mlle Cécile de Rothschild. Four years later, with their savings, bank loans, and the backing of the Cazalet family and friends, the brothers opened Le Gavroche.

Why "Le Gavroche"? Silvano Giraldin, who joined the restaurant in 1971 and is now a director of the company, explains: "Michael von Clemm, the international financier and first chairman of Le Gavroche, suggested it because he said we

My father, Albert (right), and uncle Michel at Le Gavroche soon after it opened in 1967

10

This big-eyed ragamuffin, painted by Pouc of Montmartre, was presented on our opening night. He may not be quite the character Victor Hugo had in mind, but he's a genuine Parisian gavroche

should have a typically French name that was easy to pronounce, easy to remember, and that people would talk about." He was proved right.

The two brothers, Michel and Albert, took it in turns to be in charge of the kitchen or the taking of orders in the dining room. Both are famously stubborn and thrive on fierce, if usually short-lived, arguments; one can imagine how the kitchen staff must have suffered, doing things Michel's way one week, Albert's way the next. Some of the regular customers seemed to enjoy "spotting the differences," but showed no preference, and the restaurant was always full.

Before Le Gavroche, there had been an Italian restaurant, Canova, on the same site. The maître d', Tony Battistella, was offered a job by the Roux brothers and stayed for more than 30 years, showing loyalty that is almost impossible to find in today's constantly changing catering world. Le Gavroche seems to inspire this kind of loyalty: Eddie has worked here as a dishwasher for 20 years and Albert Roux is godfather to two of his children—and hosted their christening parties at the restaurant.

It's a whole life that goes on here, and I have always been part of it. When we moved to London in 1967 I was still a little kid, and some of my earliest memories are of the smell of the kitchen, and being given petits fours as treats. Later, as a young teenager, I did dishwashing during the summer vacations to earn some money. Every Saturday night the tips were shared out and the maîtres d' would inevitably start a game of poker. Albert liked to join in and, with a cigarette hanging out of the corner of his mouth, often ended up winning all the tips!

Much is said of the dedication and skill of my father and uncle, but I think this is the place to give credit to one of the unsung heroines of Le Gavroche, my mother, Monique. She is an excellent cook, but her role was not in the kitchen. The brothers liked to serve foie gras, truffles, Bresse poultry, veal and French cheeses but, in the days before Britain joined the European Community, the problem was getting the ingredients into the country. So, two or three times a week, my mother would drive to Paris to bring back food "for her own consumption"—obviously, she had a large and hungry family! To avoid arousing suspicion, she traveled from different ports along the south coast of England and even, occasionally, from Lydd airport in Kent, where you used to be able to drive your car on to the aeroplane and drive off at Le Touquet on the other side of the Channel. At certain times of year she took prized British ingredients to fellow restaurateurs in Paris; I sometimes went with her, and I remember the suitcases filled with wild salmon and game, dripping melted ice that sloshed all over the car.

Those of you who were around in the barren culinary years of the sixties will recall that finding a good restaurant was difficult: Oversized vegetables, poorly stored fish and unimaginative cuts of meat were the order of the day—often the fault of the wholesalers who supplied the restaurants. Albert and Michel decided to go to the markets themselves, setting off at four in the morning three times a week, and sometimes I went, too. The old Covent Garden market, selling vegetables, fruit and flowers, was a nightmare as huge juggernauts from Holland blocked the narrow 18th-century streets in central London. The fish market at Billingsgate, on the other hand, was a delight and, at that time, buying from the market was the only way to guarantee the freshness of the fish; demand in Britain was so low that much of the fish went to buyers on the Continent. Times have changed and now we often get deliveries direct from the coast; in fact the traffic has reversed, and some enterprising merchants bring us fish fresh from ports in France. Smithfield, the meat market, was

This presentation plate (above), designed by Pauline Bewick, was used from 1982 to 1994

Now it is my face that smiles at guests from the presentation plates; again, the design was taken from a painting by Pauline Bewick

another story again. In order to get the cuts of meat they wanted, the brothers did much of their own butchery. In those days, the market was run by unions, and customers were meant to wait for a porter to carry their purchases. One day my father decided he could do this himself and I watched him staggering under the weight of a side of beef, with market officials running after him to try and make him use a porter; he shrugged as best he could under the circumstances, replied in French and carried on. One of the problems with Smithfields was the quality and availability of offal. Delicacies such as veal kidneys were next to impossible to come by—but they were equally difficult to sell, since in the late sixties and early seventies people didn't expect to find offal in a restaurant of this calibre. Albert and Michel continued visiting the markets for several years and, with their singleminded approach to quality, gradually persuaded their suppliers to change their attitude. Some of these same suppliers are still selling to Le Gavroche 30 years later.

With the success of Le Gavroche, Albert and Michel were soon ready to expand. In 1969 they opened London's first French-style charcuterie, Le Cochon Rose, and a restaurant in the financial district, Le Poulbot. By the late 1970s the Roux empire had grown to include four brasseries, a catering division and The Waterside Inn in Bray, Berkshire. Le Gavroche moved to Upper Brook Street in 1981 and won its third Michelin star in 1982; it was the first restaurant in the United Kingdom to achieve this, and the only one until The Waterside Inn was awarded its third Michelin star in 1985. In the late 1980s, the empire was dismantled. The two restaurants became separate companies, with Michel taking responsibility for The Waterside Inn and Albert taking over at Le Gavroche.

*The entrance to the restaurant, in
Upper Brook Street, Mayfair*

Over the past 30 years, thousands of young chefs and
waiters have been trained in the Roux ethics, and they have
since spread the knowledge and values that until Le Gavroche
opened were unheard of in British kitchens. Chefs such as
Pierre Koffmann, Christian Delteil, Christian Germain,
Rowley Leigh, Gordon Ramsay, Jean-Louis Taillebaud and
Marcus Wareing have all acknowledged their debt to the Roux

The menu (above) and wine list (opposite) designed by Paul Gaisford were used from 1994 to 1997

brothers. Equally astounding is the global network of former Gavroche staff: On vacation in Mauritius the hotel's general manager had worked for my father! We never advertise for staff. People write to us because they want to work here and learn the Roux way; some are prepared to wait two years.

I followed my father into the profession, beginning as an apprentice *pâtissier* in Paris, then working for a *charcutier* and butcher, also in Paris, followed by a spell in Hong Kong. The greatest outside influence on my work were the two years I spent working for the master chef Alain Chapel at his restaurant at Mionnay, near Lyon. I took charge at Le Gavroche when my father retired from the kitchen in 1992.

At Le Gavroche we have kept notes on all the recipes we have served since 1967, and indeed we have dishes on the menu which have been favorites for years, though there has been a change in how we cook them. In my father's day, the soufflé Suissesse, for example, was served as a double portion with lashings of cream. I serve a single portion and don't reduce the cream so much, so it is not quite as heavy. It is the same dish, but modified to the modern palate. This could be said to be a trend in French cooking in general. However, we also serve some completely classic dishes, such as the navarin of lamb, which hasn't changed in any way.

A subtle fusion with other cultures has not shaken my foundations in classic French cuisine, but is evident in the use of spices such as star anise in a lobster broth and cinnamon in a red wine sauce to go with duck. But to quote the phrase, there is nothing new under the sun, and one of the Roux brothers' original specialities was *veau à l'ananas*, veal with pineapple in a hollandaise sauce, lightly flavored with curry.

Early Gavroche menus included cream of watercress and French onion soup. Classic dishes, but you'd never find them now in a restaurant at this level, although I couldn't resist

This gavroche has made himself at home on the streets of Mayfair

including an onion soup made with cider and Calvados in this book. One item you wouldn't have found before 1973 was hot foie gras. Many uncooked foods could not be brought through customs, so although Michel and Albert cooked foie gras in terrines, they couldn't afford to draw attention to a dish as stunning as hot foie gras, fresh from the pan. However, they love its satiny, melt-in-the-mouth richness as much as I do, and were very relieved when restrictions were lifted.

Puddings have become more delicate. In the early years, many of the desserts were more like tea-time gateaux: Chocolate cake, tarte Amandine—a rich almond tart—and the brothers's speciality, La Rose du Chef, a buttery cake on a nougatine base, topped with cream and a sugar rose. Now, puddings are a light delicacy rather than a massive injection of sugar that you need to sleep off for three hours!

We change the basic menu three or four times a year, but it always balances innovations with old favorites; this way we hope to please all our customers. We have many loyal regulars who enjoy the perfection of our French haute cuisine whenever they are in London, and some of them order the same dish every time; for other customers, dinner at Le Gavroche is a once-in-a-lifetime occasion.

The pages of our visitors' book read like an international *Who's Who* of aristocracy, ambassadors, industrialists and entrepreneurs, liberally laced with stars of the stage and screen, arts, music and sport. Not every customer is invited to sign the book; for example Silvano never asks politicans or royalty. He tells the story of Diana, Princess of Wales, who ate at Le Gavroche on a number of occasions, including the day the news broke about her affair with James Hewitt. When Silvano opened the door for her to leave, seeing the pack of newshounds waiting outside, she took a deep breath and said, "Let's face the music."

Planning and preparation

The food is the star of the show, and public acclaim goes to the chefs, but I never forget the role of the supporting cast: The waiters and other front of house staff, led, at Le Gavroche, by restaurant manager Silvano Giraldin. I am pleased to say that the work of waiters and sommeliers is now being rewarded by the media, but my father and uncle recognized their importance long ago. "The Roux brothers always insisted that a good restaurant relies on an entente cordiale between the kitchen and the front of house," says Silvano.

The public face of Le Gavroche, Silvano Giraldin has been restaurant manager since 1975. A master of "les arts de la table," nothing escapes his meticulous attention to detail, from the spotless shine of every coffee spoon to the perfectly timed arrival of every dish. His memory for names, faces and customers' favorite dishes is legendary, his tact and discretion unparalleled. One story in particular bears witness to both his dedication to the unruffled running of the restaurant and his diplomatic skills. During one lunchtime service, a couple arrived, were shown to their table, and their order taken. The lady left the table and went to the ladies' room. A few minutes later, the man followed her there. Thinking quickly, Silvano advised his staff that any other ladies should be directed to another lavatory in the building until the couple reappeared. Some 45 minutes later, they did. Their lunch was

First impressions: An informal table setting on a pristine white cloth. Each place has a cheerful presentation plate, each table an ornamental silver animal or bird

served shortly afterward. And will Silvano reveal the lady's name? Never!

As any restaurant aspiring to stardom knows, the Michelin inspectors are looking for more than superb food. Their checklist includes tasteful decor, faultless table settings and, above all, impeccable service. You may ask, what has this to do with the home cook? Well, imagine that you have been invited to dinner by a new acquaintance. When you arrive, you notice a chilly atmosphere—perhaps your hosts have had an argument—and that the lighting is rather bright and unflattering, or the seating uncomfortable. No matter how excellent the food, it will be difficult to relax and fully enjoy the occasion. Each element—food, wine, surroundings and ambience—contributes to the success of the meal.

One of the most obvious ways to prepare for a dinner at home is to set the table well in advance. This will give you a chance to check you have everything you need, and will give your guests an impression of order and calm when they enter the dining room.

A classic restaurant table setting comprises a wine glass and a water glass, a basic set of silverware, side plates with butter knives and napkins, salt and pepper, and an ashtray. Each place is set with a presentation plate, and Le Gavroche "extras" include a small flower arrangement or a candle, and an ornamental silver animal or bird. Few customers realize the work that even this relatively simple setting entails—nor should they. Yet before the restaurant opens, Silvano's team spend hours cleaning, polishing, checking and polishing some more. Plates are washed twice, then given a final polish with a cloth dipped in a solution of vinegar and water to dissolve any traces of grease which might dull their gleaming surfaces. The vinegar evaporates and 2 minutes later there is absolutely no vinegary smell left. Then the plates are polished again. Glasses

The finishing touch: When everything is set out on the table, the glasses are given a final polish to make sure they are fingerprint-free and gleaming

and silverware undergo similarly stringent cleaning. Tablecloths and napkins are always freshly laundered—and rejected if they show any sign of imperfection or careless ironing, which might distract the eye and detract from the overall sensation of luxury. When the food orders are taken, the basic knives or forks will be exchanged for those appropriate to each dish: Soup spoons, fish forks, steak knives, and so on. At home, you will have the advantage over any restaurant of knowing what food you are going to serve, so you can set out the correct knives, forks and spoons.

As for table decorations, remember that these should please the eye without cluttering the table. The dinner table is not the place for huge flower arrangements: A small posy, a few choice stems or, alternatively, a simple ornament are all that's needed.

Unbelievably, our silver table decorations, weighing around 1lb, occasionally, though fortunately rarely, disappear from the restaurant with a customer. Ashtrays are always popular with souvenir hunters. They are sold at the restaurant for a small sum, but Silvano orders 1000 of these every year, and he is sure that "borrowage" accounts for far more of that number than breakage. Coffee spoons slip into pockets; our embroidered linen from the lavatories finds its way into ladies' bags; one gentleman even unscrewed one of the brass loo paper holders during dinner service—I hope he wouldn't do that if he were a guest at a private house! Don't forget that, besides the dining room, the one room everyone will visit is the bathroom, so be sure that it is stocked with fresh soap and hand towels.

Remember that your guests have come to enjoy your company, not to test your culinary skills. Don't be too ambitious: If you're a confident cook, trying out one new dish for a dinner party can be fun, but attempting three could be a recipe for disaster. No one will feel at ease if you are tense and flustered. The best way to avoid this is by careful planning. Make a timetable and follow it. Plan the use of your oven: If you have a double oven you will be able to cook two dishes at different temperatures.

If I have one word of advice above all others, it is to read your recipes thoroughly. There is no use in launching in to a recipe, only to discover that it relies on a stock or sauce that needs to be made in advance. Prepare as many ingredients as possible so that they are ready to cook: Wash and dry salads, clean fish, trim meat. Advance preparation is the secret to any restaurant cooking: Every morning we make sure we have enough of the basic stocks and sauces to last all day; many vegetables are blanched, ready for last-minute cooking; desserts are made and chilled.

Pay attention to details: If plates need to be warmed or chilled, be sure this is done.

At Le Gavroche, Silvano and his team are constantly, yet unobtrusively, on hand to make sure customers are offered canapés, drinks, bread. At home, unless you have hired domestic help, it is up to you to attend to your guests' needs. If you are entertaining as a couple, decide in advance which of you will be making sure the drinks are kept flowing, and which of you will concentrate on the food. If you are the sole host, ask a friend to keep an eye on the drinks.

One way to create a relaxed, informal atmosphere is with French family service. This means serving food such as a whole fish on a large platter, or stews and vegetables in a big dish. Serve yourself first to show guests this is what you intend, and to give an example of the size of helping they should be taking. Pass dishes to your right.

Effortless entertaining is an illusion, but with careful planning you can pull off the illusion with ease.

Selecting the wine

Selecting the wine is part of the pleasure of planning your dinner party. At Le Gavroche our wine list is, as you might expect, predominantly French, and I like to think that there is a French wine for every occasion, every type of food. It would seem that winemakers around the world agree, because so many of the wines from newer winemaking regions have been inspired by the classic wines of Bordeaux, Burgundy, the Loire and the Rhône.

The first thing to think about is the apéritif, and its importance should not be underestimated. Its role is to stimulate the appetite, arouse the taste buds and excite the senses with subtle tastes that will not mask the food that is to follow—and that is why champagne is always my first choice. As much as I enjoy a refreshing gin and tonic or a single malt whisky, they are too high in alcohol to serve as an apéritif. Not only is champagne a wonderfully convivial drink—its effervescence is infectious—it is also the perfect foil for its edible counterparts, canapés or *amuse-bouches*.

The best champagne for an apéritif is one that is light and fresh tasting; with food, a fuller style such as a vintage champagne would usually be more appropriate. Vintage champagne is best served lightly chilled, between 46 and 50°F: Any colder and some of the delicate notes will be lost. Non-vintage champagne can be served colder, at 43 to 46°F.

A glass of champagne is the perfect way to start a meal

The cellars of Le Gavroche are a wine-lover's dream come true. I have found a magnum of Krug Collection 1969 and sommelier Thierry Tomasin has a Château Latour 1967, a Premier Cru from Bordeaux, one of the great wines of the world

Be careful when opening the bottle, as a flying cork can cause a lot of damage not only to furniture but to anybody in its way. There's no real mystique involved, as long as you keep your thumb firmly on the top of the cork as you untwist the wire and carefully remove the "cage," then holding the cork firmly, tilt the bottle at an angle and gently twist the bottle until the cork pops out: The sound should resemble a sensual whisper, never a loud bang.

One of the things that makes champagne the perfect apéritif is its acidity: This helps to awaken the appetite. It is unusual these days to drink champagne throughout a meal, but certainly not unheard of; in fact I was once asked to devise a 14-course menu around the champagnes of Laurent-Perrier.

For a wine to drink before and during a meal the usual choice would be a still white wine. On a hot day in the south of France, the crisp white wines from the Coteaux du Languedoc are deliciously refreshing as an apéritif, and you would expect to drink the same wine with your meal. Remember, however, that in those idyllic circumstances you are likely to be eating light, summery food; richer food and buttery sauces would overwhelm such wines.

In summer I have always enjoyed a chilled rosé wine as an apéritif. Wine snobs tend to dismiss rosé as frivolous and barely worth the effort of uncorking, but I don't agree. The rosé wines made in the south of France are characterized by a fresh, rich nose and crisp acidity on the palate. The locals drink them throughout the summer months, and they are ideal companions to summer food—whether it is fish, meat or a salad—and outdoor living, picnics and dinners on the terrace or by the pool. The rosé wines from Coteaux d'Aix en Provence are among the best, but one of my favorites is the Tavel from the organically run Domaine de la Mordorée, near Avignon in the southern Rhône Valley. Generally speaking, rosés should be drunk within a year of release; although they can go well with food, they are primarily thirst-quenching *vins de soif*, and they don't aim to compete with the grand wines of Bordeaux or the fine, velvety wines of Burgundy.

An unusual apéritif that works equally well in summer or winter, and always keeps people guessing, is Le Communard, a popular drink in Lyon in the little cafés known as *bouchons*. It is made with young, lightly chilled Beaujolais wine and a splash of crème de cassis, and is delicious with pork or duck rillettes and toast, or an array of Lyonnais charcuterie.

I often think that too much is made of matching food and wine; so much depends on individual taste, and mood—and budget—and on the way the food is cooked and what it is served with, that there cannot possibly be a right or wrong wine for every dish. That said, there are some classic combinations that are cited so often they must be worth a try: Rich, sweet Sauternes with foie gras or strawberries; fine white Burgundy, such as Meursault, with scallops; complex, deeply flavored red wine from the Médoc, especially Pauillac, with lamb.

The subtly evolving repertoire of dishes at Le Gavroche has allowed us, over the years, to discover some especially harmonious wine and food combinations. Some of the recipes in this book are accompanied by a wine suggestion made by our head sommelier, Thierry Tomasin. These suggestions may take some tracking down from specialist wine merchants, but most are available and affordable—although one or two of them are "once in a lifetime" bottles.

If you want just one bottle to drink throughout your meal at Le Gavroche, the best thing you can do is to ask your wine waiter for advice; he or she is trained to find a good match for the various dishes you have chosen. At your own dinner parties everyone will be eating the same food, so selecting the wine is a little more straightforward. You don't necessarily have to drink white wine with fish and red with meat—such rules are made to be broken, and I would say the only rule is to trust your own judgment and drink what you enjoy. Do bear your guests' tastes in mind: Some people will always prefer red wine to white, while others avoid red wine.

Some wines seem to be good all-rounders, and go well with a wide range of foods. Dry white wines such as Alsace Riesling and Pinot Gris, or the fuller, rounder white Burgundies can take their place throughout a meal, as can some of the red wines from the Loire, such as Bourgueil, Chinon and Saumur-Champigny. Although fairly light, from good vintages these have a fine depth of fruit.

The wine list contains some rare, expensive and sometimes irreplaceable bottles, but there are also plenty of modern wines at modest prices

The style and flavors of the wine should somehow match those of the food. The richness of foie gras finds its counterpart in intensely sweet wines with the distinctive flavor of botrytis, or noble rot: These include Sauternes and Alsace Selection de Grains Nobles. A rustic terrine looks for a more straightforward partner such as a Beaujolais. Shellfish has an affinity with crisp, fresh white wines, especially those from near the sea such as Muscadet, but also with Chablis, far inland but world famous for its bone-dry wines. Smoked fish goes well with the spicy flavors of Gewurztraminer.

Avoid tannic red wines with most fish and shellfish, as the combination makes the wine taste unpleasant and metallic. This is not the same as saying that no red wine goes with fish. "Meatier" fish such as turbot, salmon and monkfish are often cooked in ways that cry out for red wine; for instance when I cook turbot in red Bandol wine I would always choose to drink the same wine. Lower tannin reds are most often found from the Loire, Burgundy and Beaujolais. The conventional choice with fish dishes is white Burgundy—the richer the sauce, the richer and older the wine should be. For lighter Burgundies look for names such as St-Véran and Pouilly-Fuissé from the Mâconnais region. Alternatives from the Rhône include Hermitage blanc and aromatic Condrieu.

Chicken, rabbit, and pork can be equally happy with white or red wine—the style of the dish is more important—but either way, Burgundy has the answer: Buttery Chardonnay will compliment a creamy sauce, and mushroom sauces are perfect with fragrant Pinot Noir.

With red meat and game, well, you could choose white wine, but I'd go for red every time. Mighty Bordeaux; rich, sensuous Burgundy; fragrant Côte-Rôtie or robust Gigondas from the Rhône or intriguing wines from the herb-scented hills of Provence and Languedoc—the choice is yours.

Finally, think about the order in which you serve your wines. If you have a star bottle of really mature wine, it is a good idea to precede it with a younger wine from the same region: Think of this as a support act, introducing the palate to a theme that will be developed as the meal progresses. To do justice to your wines and palates, serve dry wines before sweet, light before heavy, and delicately flavored wines before powerful ones.

At Le Gavroche we have a superb cellar of more than 2000 wines, including some of the greatest vintages of the 20th century. Château Haut-Brion 1959 from Bordeaux, Romanée-Conti 1971 from Burgundy are not wines you can pop out and buy from a main street liquor store—even specialist wine merchants are unlikely to have them—but they are here in our cellars, admittedly at a price that reflects their rarity! While our wine list is undoubtedly one of the best in London, you have one advantage when serving wine at home: You can match the wine to the food well in advance and condition it accordingly. Red wines can be brought gently to room temperature in your dining room; whites can be chilled for an hour or two. Pouring the wine into a decanter can help to bring out the full flavors of red wines, and full-bodied whites can also benefit from being decanted.

At the end of the meal some people like to linger over a dessert wine, others prefer to finish with a refreshing glass of champagne. At Le Gavroche we always offer coffee and a digestif: This could be Cognac or Armagnac; personally, I like an aged single malt whisky. The key is to relax after a good dinner and, whatever you like to drink, it is always a pleasure to be offered a selection of petits fours. These tiny cakes, cookies and candies may be crisp, light as air or dense and velvety rich, but their jewel-like appearance puts the crowning touch on a meal.

Treasures from our cellars: An Armagnac labeled on our thirtieth anniversary and an 1849 Sauternes, our most expensive wine, and the rarest (in fact this is the only bottle). With wines of this antiquity, there is no way of knowing whether they will be way past their best or—miraculously—perfectly delicious

Canapés,

Petits Fours

Roquefort shortbread

Makes about 50 small biscuits

¼ lb Roquefort, Stilton or Bleu
d'Auvergne
1 cup plain flour
pinch of cayenne pepper
½ cup unsalted butter, cubed, at
room temperature
1 egg yolk

Crumble the cheese with a fork. Sift the flour and cayenne together, and make a well in the center. Place the cheese, butter, and yolks in the well and work together with your fingertips, gradually mixing in the flour. Do not overwork the dough and do not worry if small lumps of cheese remain. Wrap in plastic wrap and refrigerate for at least 2 hours.

Heat the oven to 350°F. On a lightly floured surface, roll out the dough to a thickness of ⅛ in, and cut out to any shape or size you wish. Place on a non-stick baking sheet and cook until golden brown, about 12 minutes. Transfer to a wire rack to cool. The shortbread can be stored in an airtight container for 2–3 days.

Variations: Decorate before cooking by brushing lightly with egg yolk and pressing a walnut half on to each biscuit. Or sandwich biscuits together with herb-flavored cream cheese.

Potato and Gruyère soufflés

Makes 50

¾lb large potatoes
7 tablespoons heavy cream
2¼ cups Gruyère cheese, grated
2 eggs
salt, pepper, and nutmeg
50 cooked puff pastry tartlet shells
(1½in diameter)

Bake the potatoes in their skins, then leave until cool enough to handle. Heat the oven to 375°F. Bring the cream to a boil. Put the potato flesh into the bowl of an electric mixer, add the Gruyère and eggs, and beat for 30 seconds. Pour in the boiling cream, season to taste with salt, pepper, and nutmeg, then beat for a further 30 seconds or so, until there are no more lumps (you may have to scrape down the sides of the bowl to make sure the mixture is smooth).

Put the mixture into a piping bag with a plain nozzle and pipe into the pastry tartlets. Bake in the oven until lightly souffléd and golden brown, about 2 minutes. Serve at once.

FROM TOP TO BOTTOM: Roquefort shortbread, monkfish liver toast, potato and Gruyère soufflé

Monkfish liver toasts

The liver of a monkfish can be described as the foie gras of the sea; it is truly an exquisite delicacy. Although hard to find, most good fishmongers can obtain it for you, especially in early spring when it is at its best. Creamy white with orange tinges, it resembles duck and goose foie gras in shape and texture; it has a wonderful fishy taste with a smoothness and richness that is beyond compare.

To make 20–25 canapés, take a monkfish liver of approximately 10oz (some are as big as 4½lb). Lay it flat and use a small pointed knife to remove the large veins that run from top to bottom. Season with salt and pepper and then roll tightly in plastic wrap; tie securely with string at each end and four times along the "sausage". Poach in salted simmering water for 12 minutes, then let cool until the water is hand hot. Remove from the water and refrigerate for 6 hours, until firm.

Toast thin slices of baguette or dill bread on both sides and place a generous slice of the monkfish liver on the toast. Sprinkle a few drops of lemon juice and some thinly sliced scallion on top.

Dill bread

Makes 2 loaves

½ cake compressed yeast

½–1 cup warm water

1 cup cottage cheese

1 egg

5 ¼ cups all-purpose flour

1 teaspoon baking powder

3 tablespoons butter, melted
and cooled

1 tablespoon salt

2 tablespoons caster sugar

1 onion, finely chopped

2 bunches of dill, chopped

This is wonderful with cured fish such as smoked salmon,
as well as with monkfish liver.

Dissolve the yeast in 3 tablespoons of the warm water in the
bowl of an electric mixer. Add the cottage cheese, egg, flour,
baking powder, and another 3–4 tablespoons of water, and
knead with the dough hook attachment for 3 minutes. Then
add the melted butter, salt, and sugar and continue kneading
the dough for 6 minutes, adding a little more water if
necessary; the dough should be elastic yet fairly loose. Mix in
the onion and dill, divide between two buttered 9 x 4½in loaf
pans, cover, and leave in a warm place until almost doubled in
size, about 1 hour.

Heat the oven to 350°F. Bake the bread for 25 minutes,
or until well risen and golden. Let cool slightly before taking
out of the pans; leave on a wire rack to cool completely.
Best eaten toasted, this bread can be stored in the refrigerator
for 2–3 days.

Vegetables à la grecque

Serves 50 as an *amuse-bouche*;
8 as a side dish

½lb baby artichokes (preferably
the variety called "violets"),
trimmed
2⅓ cups button onions, peeled
½lb cauliflower flowerets
½lb celery, cut into batons
2 cups button mushrooms, cleaned
⅔ cup virgin olive oil
20 sprigs of thyme
3 garlic cloves, chopped
2 teaspoons crushed cilantro seeds
2 pinches of saffron strands
salt and coarsely ground pepper
1 cup dry white wine
½ cup water
juice of 1½ lemons
3 large tomatoes, peeled, deseeded,
and chopped
1 bunch of basil

Cheesecloth bag containing:
1 tablespoon crushed cilantro seeds
1 tablespoon white peppercorns
2 cloves
1 sprig of rosemary
10 sprigs of thyme
10 sprigs of basil

Sweat the vegetables with the olive oil in a wide, thick-bottomed pan, without letting them color. Add the thyme leaves, garlic, cilantro seeds, saffron, salt, pepper, and the cheesecloth bag, and cook for 2 minutes, then add the wine, water, and lemon juice. Cover with a piece of wax paper and simmer gently until the vegetables are just cooked but still a little bit crunchy, about 8–10 minutes. Stir in the chopped tomatoes and shredded basil leaves, check the seasoning, and let cool.

Serve on spoons as a pre-dinner *amuse-bouche*, or as a vegetable dish to take on a picnic.

Spicy fig chutney

Makes about 3lb

1lb 2oz Bramley apples
⅔ cup soft brown sugar
1 cup white wine vinegar
1 red chili, finely chopped
1 teaspoon salt
1 teaspoon crushed black pepper
½ teaspoon crushed cilantro seeds
16 purple figs, quartered

Peel, core, and coarsely grate the apples, then place in a large, thick-bottomed, non-aluminum saucepan. Add the sugar, vinegar, chili, and salt, and bring to a boil, stirring frequently to prevent sticking. When almost dry, add the spices and figs, cover with a lid, and cook for 30 minutes over low heat, stirring occasionally.

Store in sterilized glass jars in a cool place or refrigerator for up to 6 months.

Bacon cornbread

Makes about 60 canapés

5 strips smoked bacon
3½oz all-purpose flour
2 teaspoons baking powder
1 teaspoon salt
2 cups polenta (yellow cornmeal)
1 egg, beaten
1½ cups buttermilk
3 tablespoons maple syrup

These can be served plain or with a little cream cheese piped on top. Cornbread can also be made in Yorkshire pudding pans and served as an accompaniment to soups or stews.

Heat the oven to 375°F. Blanch the bacon in boiling water for 1 minute, then cut into very small lardons. Fry in a non-stick pan with a tiny drop of vegetable oil until slightly crisp. Let cool with the bacon fat in the pan.

Sift the flour, baking powder, and salt into a bowl, add the cornmeal, egg, and buttermilk and beat with a wooden spoon until smooth. Fold in the maple syrup and bacon, including its fat. Pour this mixture into well buttered small cake pans, 1in diameter, and cook for 10–15 minutes, or until firm to the touch and a knife pulls out clean when inserted into the center. These should be eaten on the day they are made.

*ON THE LEFT: Vegetables à la grecque with a morsel of poached lobster.
ON THE RIGHT: Spicy fig chutney with pan-fried foie gras*

Pork rillettes

Makes about 60 canapés

14oz pork fat

2¼lbs lean pork shoulder and neck

14oz belly pork

1 onion

1 carrot

1 celery stalk

2 garlic cloves

1 bouquet garni with 10 sage leaves

7fl oz dry white wine

salt and white pepper

Always choose the best quality organic pork as it really does make a difference to the flavour.

Dice the pork fat into ½ in cubes and place in a thick-bottomed saucepan; add just enough cold water to cover. Bring to a boil, then simmer for 1 hour.

By now most of the fat should be soft and translucent. Add all the meat, cut into ¾ in cubes, then add the whole (peeled) onion, carrot, celery, and garlic, and the bouquet garni, 3½ fl oz of wine, salt, and pepper. Bring to a boil, cover with a piece of wax paper, and simmer for 1½ hours, stirring occasionally. Add a little water from time to time if the mixture becomes dry.

When cooked, the meat should be so soft and tender it crumbles to the touch. Add the remaining wine and let cool for 1 hour.

Transfer the contents of the pan to a clean bowl set over a bowl of ice. Remove the bouquet garni, celery, carrot, and onion (the garlic will have "melted" into the liquid). Put on a pair of surgical gloves and break the meat up using your fingers; do this until the meat is almost white, as the fat sets. Check the seasoning, remembering that this is served cold and needs to be highly seasoned. Transfer to a clean container, cover with plastic wrap, and refrigerate. Rillettes can be stored in the refrigerator for 2 weeks if you can keep away from it!

Serve with toasted sourdough or rye bread and a dandelion salad as a canapé or first course.

Pissaladière

Makes 30 canapés

4 large onions
2 tablespoons olive oil
1 bay leaf
3–4 sprigs of thyme
salt and pepper
½lb puff pastry (page 278)
1 egg, beaten
30 black olives (preferably the small variety from Nice)
12 anchovy fillets

Peel the onions, cut in half, and slice very thinly. Heat the oil in a large, thick-bottomed saucepan over medium heat; add the onions, bay leaf, and thyme, and season lightly with salt, generously with pepper. Cook for 35–40 minutes, stirring frequently, until the onions are very tender, sweet, and light brown in color. Let cool.

Roll out the pastry dough to a thickness of ⅛ in and cut into 2in wide strips, the same length as your baking sheet. Fold each side over by ½ in to make the borders. Prick the center with a fork and lightly brush the edges with beaten egg. Refrigerate for 1 hour.

Heat the oven to 425°F. Spread the onions thickly along the center of the pastry strips, arrange the olives and thin slivers of anchovy on top, and cook for about 15 minutes, until the dough is light golden. Serve warm, cut into bite-sized pieces, brushed with a little extra virgin olive oil.

Pickled wild mushrooms

To fill a 1 quart preserving jar

5 cups wild mushrooms (e.g., ceps,
chanterelles, shiitake)
2 cups white wine vinegar
1 ¼ cups light brown sugar
2 tablespoons coarse sea salt
1 tablespoon black peppercorns
3 garlic cloves, crushed
3 whole cloves
3–4 sprigs of herbs (optional)

In the south of France everyone has their own recipe for preserving wild mushrooms. Small ceps are best in this recipe. Serve as a pre-dinner nibble, or as part of a picnic, with a few pieces of dried tomatoes (page 273) if you like.

Trim and wipe clean the mushrooms. Boil the vinegar, sugar, salt, lightly crushed peppercorns, garlic, and cloves for 2 minutes, then add the mushrooms—and herbs (e.g. thyme, bay leaves, rosemary) if using—and boil gently for 6 minutes. Pour into a scrupulously clean preserving jar and seal. Store in a cool place for at least 2 weeks before eating.

Fougasse

Makes 1 large loaf

¾ cake of compressed yeast
1 ½ cups warm water
4 ½ cups bread flour
1 teaspoon salt
4 tablespoons olive oil
⅓ cup good-quality olives, pitted
and cut in half
1 egg, beaten
coarse sea salt

This Mediterranean-style flat olive bread is excellent with tapenade or vegetables à la grecque, or with vegetable soups.

Dissolve the yeast in a little warm water in a large bowl. Add the flour, salt, most of the water, and the olive oil, and knead until the dough is smooth and very elastic, about 10 minutes. Cover with a damp cloth and let rise in a warm place until doubled in size, about 1 hour.

Knead the dough briefly and add the olives. Roll out on a floured surface to form a ¾in thick leaf shape. Place on a baking sheet and then, using a sharp knife, cut six slits in the dough and open them up so you can see the baking sheet. Cover with a damp cloth and let rise in a warm place.

Heat the oven to 475°F. Brush the dough lightly with beaten egg, sprinkle with coarse salt, and bake for 9 minutes, until golden brown. Let cool on a wire rack.

RIGHT:Pickled wild mushrooms

Dill and crab pancakes

Makes 16 pancakes;

6–8 canapés per pancake

1lb 2oz crab claw meat
bunch of dill, roughly chopped
2 shallots, finely chopped
mayonnaise, tomato ketchup,
brandy, Tabasco sauce

Pancakes
3 eggs
1 cup plain flour
6 tablespoons wholewheat flour
scant 1 cup milk
1 cup water
1 tablespoon chopped fresh dill
salt and pepper

To make the pancakes, beat the eggs with a whisk and gradually beat in the remaining ingredients. Pass through a coarse sieve and let rest for at least 1 hour.

Heat a small non-stick frying pan (7in diameter), brush lightly with oil, and pour in just enough batter to coat the bottom of the pan. Cook over medium-high heat, then flip over using a palette knife, and cook the other side. Stack the pancakes between sheets of wax paper and let cool.

Pick through the crab meat to remove any bones and pieces of shell, then mix with the dill, shallots, and mayonnaise, adding ketchup, brandy, and Tabasco to taste. Spread the crab mixture over the pancakes and roll up to form cigar shapes; trim the edges and place in the refrigerator until needed. Using a very sharp knife, slice into bite-sized pieces.

Pumpkin fritters

Makes 15–20 fritters

about 1 ½ lb pumpkin
1 cup all-purpose flour
3 teaspoons baking powder
1 tablespoon caster sugar
½ teaspoon Chinese 5-spice
powder
1 egg
oil for deep-frying

Cut the pumpkin into large chunks, discarding the skin and seeds. Bake in a hot oven until tender. Let cool; you should have about ½ lb cooked pumpkin. Sift the flour with the baking powder.

Mash the pumpkin together with the sugar, spice, and egg, using a potato masher or in a blender. When well mixed, fold in the flour and baking powder.

Drop heaping teaspoonfuls of the mixture into hot oil (360°F) in a deep-frying pan and cook until puffed and browned underneath; carefully turn with a fork and continue to cook until golden all over. Drain on paper towels and sprinkle with salt. Serve warm.

Tapenade

Makes about 1lb

1 ½ oz anchovy fillets
½ cup black olives, pitted
½ cup green olives, pitted
½ cup capers, drained
scant 1 cup extra virgin olive oil
1 lemon
freshly ground black pepper

This appetizing olive, caper, and anchovy spread originates in Provence. Serve as a dip with raw vegetables, or spread thinly on toast, accompanied by a glass of chilled rosé wine.

Rinse the anchovies under cold water and pat dry. Put the anchovies in a blender with the olives, capers, and olive oil, and blend until smooth. Add lemon juice and pepper to taste. This can be stored in an airtight container in the refrigerator for 10–14 days.

Ginger brandy snaps

Makes 20–25

½ cup unsalted butter, softened
1 ¼ cups caster sugar
¼ cup light corn syrup
1 cup all-purpose flour, sifted
ground ginger, to taste

Mix the butter, sugar, light corn syrup, and flour in an electric mixer with the paddle beater attachment for 5 minutes or until smooth. Refrigerate for 24 hours.

Heat the oven to 350°F. Spread the paste thinly on a lightly greased non-stick baking sheet and cook until it is a caramel brown color, about 8 minutes.

Let cool on the baking sheet for a few seconds, then cut out circles using a pastry cutter. Transfer to a wire rack to cool and firm up. Alternatively, drape the warm brandy snaps over a rolling pin to give a *tuile* shape, or place into cup-cake cups to form a basket in which to serve ice cream or berries.

Coconut tuiles

Makes about 30

3 eggs
1 ¼ cups caster sugar
3 cups unsweetened shredded coconut

Heat the oven to 325°F. Whisk the eggs and sugar until just mixed, then add the coconut and continue whisking until smooth. Spacing them well apart, drop teaspoonfuls of the mixture on to a lightly greased non-stick baking sheet and spread out very thinly using the back of a fork dipped in water. Alternatively, press the mixture into a round cutter, using moistened fingertips, to make perfect circles. Cook until pale brown, about 12 minutes. Using a palette knife, transfer to a wire rack and let cool.

TOP TIER, LEFT TO RIGHT: Ginger brandy snap, Coconut tuile, Poppy and sesame seed tuile.
BOTTOM TIER, CLOCKWISE FROM LEFT: Raspberry macaroon, Lemon macaroon,
Chocolate macaroon, Almond and raisin petit four, Cilantro tuile

Pepper tuiles

Makes about 30

⅔ cup unsalted butter, softened

1¼ cups caster sugar

7fl oz canned coconut milk

1 teaspoon cracked black pepper

1 teaspoon cracked
Szechwan pepper

3½oz all-purpose flour

Mix the butter, sugar, and coconut milk with a whisk. When smooth, add the peppers and fold in the flour. Let rest in the refrigerator for at least 1 hour.

Heat the oven to 350°F. Spread the mixture very thinly on a non-stick baking sheet and cook until light golden, 8–10 minutes.

While still warm, cut out circles and let cool on a sheet of wax paper; alternatively, drape the warm circles over a rolling pin to set into *tuile* shapes. The tuiles can be stored for several days in an airtight container.

Honey and thyme tuiles

Makes about 40

1½ cups light brown sugar

1¼ cups flower-scented
clear honey

1½ cups all-purpose flour

3½fl oz warm water

¾ cup unsalted butter, softened

3 teaspoons fresh thyme leaves

Put the sugar, honey, flour, and water into the bowl of an electric mixer and whisk at low speed until smooth, then add the softened butter and thyme. Refrigerate for at least 1 hour.

Heat the oven to 375°F. Spread the mixture thinly on a non-stick baking sheet, then cook until pale brown, about 6 minutes.

While still warm, cut out circles and either let cool on a sheet of wax paper or drape the warm circles over a rolling pin to set into *tuile*s.

Honey tuiles

Makes about 30

⅔ cup unsalted butter
1 cup light brown sugar
½ cup flower-scented clear honey
1 ¾ cups all-purpose flour
5 egg whites

Put the butter, sugar, and honey in a saucepan over low heat until they melt together. Let cool slightly, then whisk in the flour and egg whites. Refrigerate for at least 1 hour.

Heat the oven to 350°F. Spread the mixture very thinly on a non-stick baking sheet. Cook until pale brown, 8–10 minutes. While still warm, cut out circles and let cool on a sheet of wax paper.

Cilantro tuiles

Makes about 20

½ cup unsalted butter, softened
1 ¼ cups caster sugar
½ cup light corn syrup
1 cup all-purpose flour
3 teaspoons finely crushed cilantro seeds

Mix the butter, sugar, light corn syrup, and flour in an electric mixer with the paddle beater attachment for 5 minutes or until smooth. Refrigerate for 24 hours.

Heat the oven to 350°F. Spread the mixture as thinly as possible on a non-stick baking sheet, and sprinkle liberally with the crushed cilantro seeds. Cook until light brown, about 8 minutes. While still warm, cut out circles and drape over a rolling pin to set into *tuiles*.

Sesame and poppy tuiles

Makes about 30

⅔ cup unsalted butter
⅔ cup caster sugar
¼ cup glucose syrup
3 tablespoons milk
2 cups sesame seeds
¼ cup poppy seeds

Put the butter, sugar, glucose syrup, and milk into a saucepan over low heat, stirring continuously until they melt together. Fold in the sesame and poppy seeds and let cool.

Heat the oven to 400°F. Spread the mixture thinly on a non-stick baking sheet. Cook until golden, about 6–8 minutes. While still warm, cut out circles or other shapes and let cool on a sheet of wax paper.

Pistachio madeleines

Makes 36 small madeleines,
12 larger ones

2 eggs
¼ cup caster sugar
2 teaspoons pistachio paste
(optional)
½ cup all-purpose flour
1 teaspoon baking powder
4 tablespoons unsalted butter,
melted
¼ cup chopped peeled pistachio
nuts

Lightly beat the eggs with the sugar and pistachio paste, if using, just enough to incorporate the sugar. Fold in the sifted flour and baking powder, then the pistachios and melted butter; do not overwork. Let rest for 1 hour.

Heat the oven to 425°F. Butter and flour the madeleine molds: These are normally sold as trays of 18 for petits fours size or 6 for larger madeleines.

Using a piping bag or spoon, three-quarters fill each mold. Cook for 5 minutes for small madeleines, 10 minutes for larger ones; do not overcook as they should remain moist. As soon as they are cooked tip the madeleines out of the molds on to a wire rack to cool. They are at their best when eaten within the hour.

Lemon madeleines
Replace the pistachio paste and nuts with the grated zest and juice of 1 lemon and, if you like, 2 drops of lemon extract.

Orange madeleines
Replace the pistachio paste and nuts with the grated zest and juice of ½ an orange.

Whisky truffles

Makes 50

1 ¼ cups whipping cream
2lb 6oz bitter chocolate (62%
cocoa solids), chopped
1 ¼ cups whisky
8–10 tablespoons unsweetened
cocoa powder

Bring the cream to a boil, remove from the heat, and stir in the chocolate until completely melted, then whisk in the whisky. Set the mixture over a bowl of ice and continue whisking until almost set. Spread in a tray in a 1in deep layer, cover, and refrigerate for at least 3 hours.

Using a Parisienne spoon or small melon baller dipped in hot water, scoop out your truffles. Roll these in cocoa powder and then refrigerate for at least 1 hour before serving.

For a professional finish you can dip the truffles in melted couverture chocolate before dredging in cocoa powder. If you do this, make sure the truffles are completely set before dipping in the melted chocolate.

Almond and raisin petits fours with whisky and honey

Makes 36

1 ¼ cups unsalted butter
10 egg whites
1 ¼ cups caster sugar
1 cup ground almonds
1 cup all-purpose flour
¾ cup golden raisins, blanched in
boiling water
4 tablespoons honey
4 tablespoons whisky

Heat the oven to 425°F. Butter and flour small cake pans 1in diameter and ¾ in deep. Heat the butter until it turns light brown—"noisette" stage—and let cool.

Whisk the egg whites with the sugar until frothy but not stiff. Fold in the almonds and flour and, when smooth, fold in the butter, including any brown bits. Fill the cake pans two-thirds full, and dot a few golden raisins into each one. Cook for 10 minutes, until the cakes are risen and golden.

Stir the honey and whisky together over low heat. As they come out of the oven, generously brush the hot cakes with the honey and whisky mixture.

Macaroons

Makes 30–40

*1 cup unsweetened ground
almonds*
2 cups confectioner's sugar
4 egg whites
1 ½ tablespoons caster sugar

Heat the oven to 350°F. Pass the ground almonds and confectioner's sugar through a fine sieve (add a tablespoon of cocoa powder to make chocolate macaroons). Whisk the egg whites until frothy, then add the caster sugar, and whisk until stiff. Lightly fold the almond mixture into the egg whites: The mixture should be very smooth and quite soft.

Using a piping bag with a size 8 (½in) nozzle, pipe little blobs ½in wide on to a baking sheet lined with non-stick baking paper (you could also use a teaspoon, but this takes a lot longer). Cook for 15 minutes, then let cool on the baking sheet; the macaroons should be crisp on the outside yet remain a little soft in the center.

When cold, remove from the paper and sandwich two macaroons together with vanilla-flavored crème pâtissière (page 280); for chocolate macaroons, use chocolate ganache.

Variations: For raspberry macaroons, put a drop of red food coloring in the egg whites and sandwich with a good raspberry jam. For lemon macaroons, use yellow food coloring and fill with lemon-flavored crème pâtissière.

Chocolate ganache

⅓ cup heavy cream
½lb plain chocolate, chopped
*⅓ cup unsalted butter, at room
temperature*

Boil the cream for 2 minutes, then let cool slightly. Melt the chocolate in a bowl over a saucepan of simmering water. Pour the warm cream into the chocolate, whisking continuously, and beat until smooth. Leave until lukewarm.

Beat the butter, preferably with an electric whisk, until very light and creamy. Still beating, add the chocolate mixture a little at a time, until the mixture is smooth and shiny.

Breton shortbread

Makes 16

2¼ cups all-purpose flour
pinch of salt
1 cup plus 2 tablespoons unsalted
butter, cubed, at room temperature
½ cup caster sugar
2 egg yolks
1 tablespoon crème fraîche
2 teaspoons vanilla extract
1 small egg, beaten

The beauty of this shortbread lies in its richness and crumbly texture; it is very fragile when cooked.

Sift the flour and salt on to a clean work surface and make a well in the center. Put the butter, sugar, yolks, cream, and vanilla into the well and, using your fingertips, mix the center ingredients together without overworking. When evenly mixed, start bringing in the flour, again using only the fingertips with delicate movements. Once all the flour has been incorporated, bring the dough together in a ball, wrap in plastic wrap and refrigerate for at least 2 hours.

Heat the oven to 350°F. Roll out the dough (avoid using too much flour) to just less than ¼in thick and cut out 1½in rounds. Brush lightly with beaten egg and decorate with a fork. Cook on a baking sheet lined with wax paper until pale golden, 15–18 minutes. Let cool a little on the baking sheet before placing on a wire rack to cool completely.

Hazelnut shortbread

Makes 30

⅓ cup skinned hazelnuts
¾ cup unsalted butter, softened
¾ cup confectioner's sugar, sifted
2¼ cups all-purpose flour, sifted
pinch of salt

Lightly toast the hazelnuts under a broiler, let cool, then roughly chop. Mix the butter with the confectioner's sugar, then, using your fingertips, gently mix in the flour, salt, and hazelnuts. Roll the dough into cylinders, 1in diameter, wrap in plastic wrap and refrigerate for at least 2 hours; this dough can also be frozen and baked on another day.

Heat the oven to 350°F. Cut ¼in thick slices off the dough and cook on a non-stick baking sheet for 15–18 minutes, until golden. These can be left plain or, when cold, they can be decorated with melted chocolate.

Asparagus Baby lamb
Lima beans Morel
Sorrel St G
Wild s

Poached lobster in Chardonnay broth flavored with orange and star anise

Serves 6

6 quarts court bouillon (page
266) made with Chardonnay wine
6 Scottish lobsters
(1–1lb 2oz each)
2 sprigs of flat-leaf parsley
1 orange
2 small onions
1 carrot
18 star anise pods
2 tablespoons crème fraîche
(optional)

Strain 1 quart of the court bouillon through a cheesecloth-lined sieve and set aside. Bring the remaining court bouillon to a boil in a large saucepan and cook the lobsters in this for 5 minutes. Remove from the heat and leave the lobsters in the liquid for 10 minutes.

Pick off the parsley leaves and blanch in boiling salted water for 20 seconds. Refresh in ice-cold water, drain and set aside.

Peel the orange with a vegetable peeler, taking care not to remove any of the white pith. Cut the zest into very thin strips (julienne). Place in a small saucepan of cold water, bring to a boil, then drain and refresh in cold water. Repeat the process three times; drain and set aside.

Peel the onions and cut into rings. Peel the carrot and run a cannelle knife along the length of the carrot five times, then slice into flower-shaped circles.

Split the lobsters in half lengthwise. Crack the claws, pick out the claw meat, and place in the head cavity.

Bring the strained court bouillon to a boil and add the onion, carrot, star anise, and orange julienne. Boil for 3 minutes, until the vegetables are tender but still a little crunchy. If you like, you can add the crème fraîche and froth the liquid with a hand blender. Finally, add the parsley.

Place the two halves of a lobster in each soup plate and pour the hot liquid over them.

Wine suggestion:
Lirac 'Cuvée de la Reine des Bois'
1999, Domaine de la Mordorée

Wild salmon with St George's mushrooms

Serves 6

1½lb St George's mushrooms
(choose small ones if possible)
3 shallots, chopped
⅔ cup butter
salt and pepper
2 tablespoons dry white wine
⅓ cup fish stock (page 266)
1 tablespoon heavy cream
6 wild salmon steaks
(about 5oz each), skin on
olive oil
12 medium leeks
18 dried tomato halves
(page 273), cut into strips
½ lemon

St George's Day is on 23 April and that is when the sweet-scented mushrooms of the same name begin to appear all over Britain. St George's mushrooms (*Tricholoma georgii*) are called *mousserons* in French; they look like commercially grown mushrooms except that they are completely white. By the month of May they are at their best—and so is wild salmon.

Trim the stalks off the mushrooms. If necessary, wash the mushrooms very briefly; do not let soak.

Sweat the shallots in 2 tablespoons of the butter. When they are soft, add the mushrooms, and season with salt and pepper. Cook gently for 5 minutes, or until the mushrooms release their liquid. Add the wine and boil for 2 minutes. Add the fish stock and boil for 3 minutes, then stir in the cream followed by the remaining butter, cut into small cubes, to make a glossy sauce.

Heat the oven to 375°F. In a non-stick ovenproof pan, cook the salmon skin side down in a few drops of olive oil over high heat. When the skin is nicely browned, put the pan in the oven for 6 minutes; this keeps the flesh pink and moist.

Trim the leeks and cut the white ends to make 3½in lengths. Rinse in cold water and then cook in boiling salted water until just tender. Drain thoroughly, then cut into four lengthwise, and place on serving plates. Put the salmon steaks on top of the leeks. Add the strips of tomato to the sauce, together with a few drops of lemon juice if needed, and reheat gently. Spoon the mushrooms and sauce around the fish.

Wine suggestion:
Meursault 'La Pièce sous le Bois' 1982,
Robert Ampeau

Breton fish and lobster stew

Serves 6

*lobster bisque (page 212) without
the cream or Armagnac
2 lobsters (1lb 5oz each)
6 red mullet fillets (2–2½oz
each)
6 pieces of turbot (2–2½oz each)
2 large carrots
1 head of celery, with leaves
12 baby onions
olive oil
½ cup butter
12 button mushrooms
18 very small new potatoes
(preferably Jersey Royals), peeled
1½ tablespoons hazelnut oil*

Follow the recipe for lobster bisque and reduce by one-third to concentrate the flavor.

Cook the lobsters in heavily salted boiling water for 8 minutes. Drain, and when cool enough to handle, break off the heads. Crack the claws and remove part of the shell to reveal the meat. Cut the bodies into four equal parts with a heavy knife. Check that the fish is free of scales and bones.

Trim the carrots to make 12 even barrel shapes, then cook in boiling salted water until just tender. Remove the outer celery stalks, leaving the tender heart. Cut the celery heart into six even pieces. Fry the baby onions gently in a little oil and butter until golden all over. Fry the mushrooms in a little butter until just tender.

To finish the dish, bring the lobster bisque to a boil in a casserole dish that will be brought to the table. Put the potatoes into the lobster bisque and simmer until the potatoes are tender.

Add the remaining butter, cut into small pieces; this, with the natural starch of the potatoes, will thicken the sauce. Add the celery, cooked carrots, onions, and mushrooms to the casserole dish to reheat, then add the lobster and fish. Shake the casserole dish gently to settle the ingredients, then cover with a lid and let steam for about 1 minute. Drizzle the hazelnut oil over the casserole dish and serve immediately.

Wine suggestion:
*Pouilly-Fumé 'Silex' 1998,
Didier Dagueneau*

74

Roast salmon with spicy chorizo and aïoli

Serves 6

6–8 new potatoes (e.g., Charlotte,
Belle de Fontenay)
1 ½ cups shelled lima beans
6 Little Gem lettuces
about 2½ cups veal stock
(page 264)
2 teaspoons caster sugar
salt and pepper
olive oil
6 salmon pieces (6oz each),
skin on
30 thin slices of spicy chorizo

Boil the potatoes in salted water until tender. Drain, peel, cut into thick slices, and keep warm.

Boil the lima beans in salted water until tender. Refresh in ice-cold water, then remove the outer skins to reveal the tender bright green beans.

Blanch the lettuces in boiling salted water for 3 minutes. Refresh in ice-cold water and squeeze dry. Put the lettuces in a wide pan with the stock, sugar, salt, and pepper, and boil until the stock has thickened enough to coat the lettuce lightly; turn and baste the lettuce frequently as it cooks. Keep warm.

Heat the oven to 350°F. Heat a non-stick frying pan until very hot. Add a drop of olive oil and cook the salmon, skin side down, until browned. Turn over and cook the other side; this should take no more than 2–3 minutes on each side. The skin should be crispy yet the fish should remain very pink.

Warm the potato slices, lima beans, and chorizo in the oven for a couple of minutes.

To serve: Put a lettuce in the center of each plate with some of its cooking liquid. Arrange the lima beans, chorizo, and potato slices around the lettuce. Drizzle generously with aïoli, then lay the salmon, skin side up, on top of the lettuce.

Aïoli

5 garlic cloves
2 egg yolks
1 teaspoon Dijon mustard
2 teaspoons white wine vinegar
salt and cayenne pepper
9 fl oz light olive oil
1–2 tablespoons cold water

Peel the garlic and slice the cloves lengthwise, removing any green shoots. Put the garlic in a blender with the yolks, mustard, vinegar, salt, and cayenne pepper, and blend at full speed. Gradually trickle in the olive oil while the blender is running. After half of the oil has been incorporated stop and scrape down the sides of the blender with a rubber spatula. Continue to trickle in the oil, scraping the sides of the blender once or twice more, and adding the water with the last of the oil to thin the consistency slightly, until you have a smooth garlic mayonnaise.

Roast John Dory, artichokes barigoule

Serves 2

1 John Dory (2¼lb)
2 tablespoons olive oil
2 sprigs each of thyme and
rosemary
salt

Heat the oven to 425°F. Scale and fillet the fish, remove the pin bones using a pair of tweezers, rinse the fish, and dry with paper towel. Score the skin several times with a sharp knife to prevent the fish from curling during cooking.

Heat a non-stick ovenproof pan until smoking hot. Add the olive oil, thyme, and rosemary, then add the fish, skin side down, season, and cook over high heat for 2 minutes. Place in the hot oven for 5 minutes. Using a spatula or palette knife, gently turn the fish over and return to the oven for 3 minutes.

For an informal presentation, serve the fish in the same pan in which you have cooked the artichokes. Serve a side dish of olive oil mashed potatoes (page 231).

Artichokes barigoule

6 baby artichokes, preferably the
variety called "violets"
1 lemon, cut in half
2 slices of Bayonne or Parma ham,
diced
½ small fennel bulb
½ carrot
½ onion
⅓ cup olive oil
1 garlic clove, chopped
1 teaspoon thyme leaves
7fl oz dry white wine
salt and coarsely ground pepper
¼ cup warm water
12 basil leaves

Trim the artichokes by cutting off the outer leaves and peeling the stalk; the result should look like a lollipop. As you peel, rub the artichokes with a lemon half to prevent discoloring.

Cut the ham, fennel, carrot, and onion into small dice. Heat a thick-bottomed saucepan, add 2 tablespoons of olive oil and cook the ham until starting to brown, stirring frequently. Add the vegetables, garlic, and thyme, and cook, stirring, for a further 5 minutes.

Add the artichokes to the pan together with the wine, the juice of half a lemon, salt, and pepper, and bring to a boil. Pour in the water, cover loosely with wax paper, and cook until the artichokes are tender, about 12 minutes, turning occasionally to ensure even cooking. Just before serving mix in the remaining olive oil and freshly shredded basil leaves.

Wild sea trout with asparagus and bacon, light herb butter sauce

Serves 8

2 wild sea trout (6½–7lb each)
48 spears of (ideally) English
asparagus
12 thin strips of smoked bacon
olive oil
salt and pepper
aged balsamic vinegar
2–3 tablespoons mixed fresh
chives, chervil and tarragon

Wild sea trout from Northern Ireland comes into season at the same time as English asparagus, and this is a marriage of these two ingredients when they are at their best. Serve with Jersey Royal potatoes.

Scale and fillet the sea trout, remove the pin bones using a pair of tweezers, rinse in cold water and dry with paper towels. Cut each fillet into two portions.

Peel and trim the asparagus, then cook in boiling salted water until tender. Refresh in ice-cold water to set the color.

Make the beurre blanc and keep warm. Gently reheat the tomato fondue. Broil the bacon until crisp.

In a non-stick pan over medium heat, roll the asparagus tips with a little olive oil until warmed through. Season, add a few drops of balsamic vinegar, and remove from the heat.

Heat a non-stick frying pan, add a little olive oil, and cook the sea trout; it cooks in a matter of seconds, depending on thickness, but 30 seconds each side is usually enough. Season lightly with salt and pepper.

Arrange the asparagus on serving plates with the sea trout, tomato fondue, and finally the crispy bacon. At the very last moment add some freshly chopped herbs to the beurre blanc and pour around the asparagus.

Tomato fondue

5 plum tomatoes
2 beef tomatoes
3 shallots, finely chopped
1 tablespoon olive oil
2 garlic cloves, chopped
1 teaspoon tomato paste
1 bouquet garni, with
basil stalks added
salt and pepper

Score a cross in the tomato skins and blanch in boiling water for 15 seconds. Refresh in ice-cold water, then peel. Cut in half and remove the pips, then chop the tomato flesh.

Sweat the shallots in the olive oil over medium heat. When the shallots are soft, add the garlic, and cook for 2 minutes. Add the chopped tomatoes, tomato paste, bouquet garni, and seasoning. Cover with wax paper and cook for 1 hour, stirring occasionally until thick and almost dry.

Beurre blanc

⅓ cup dry white wine
1 tablespoon white wine vinegar
2 shallots, finely chopped
3 tablespoons heavy cream
¾ cup very cold unsalted
butter, cubed
salt and pepper
½ lemon

Bring the wine, vinegar, and shallots to a boil and reduce by half. Then add the cream and boil for 1 minute. Lower the heat and gradually whisk in the cubes of cold butter.

I like to keep the shallots in the sauce, but if you prefer a smooth finish pass the sauce through a fine sieve. Check the seasoning and add a little lemon juice to taste.

Bresse chicken with Dublin bay prawns

Serves 4

1 Bresse chicken (about 3lb)

salt and pepper

2 tablespoons olive oil

¼ cup unsalted butter

16 langoustines

1 onion, chopped

⅓ cup Madeira

1 cup chicken stock (page 264)

4 ripe tomatoes, peeled, deseeded, and diced

2¾ cups heavy cream

1 black truffle (optional)

Cut the chicken into joints: Two breasts, two legs, two thighs. Season with salt and pepper. Heat the olive oil with the butter in a sauté pan and, when foaming, add the chicken. Cook for 15 minutes, turning twice, until golden and cooked through.

Cook the langoustines in salted boiling water for 2 minutes or less, depending on size. Drain and, when cool, remove the heads and shell the tails, reserving the shells.

Remove the chicken from the pan and keep warm. Discard half of the cooking fat, add the onion to the pan, and cook until lightly browned. Add the langoustine heads and shells and crush with a wooden spoon, keeping the pan over low heat. Deglaze with the Madeira, then add the stock and tomatoes and cook until nearly dry. Add the cream, bring to a boil, and reduce to a light sauce consistency. Pass through a fine sieve into a clean pan.

Reheat the chicken and langoustine tails in the sauce, taking care not to let it boil or the langoustines will become tough. Serve immediately, with fresh pasta. As a treat, garnish with sliced cooked truffle.

Wine suggestion:
Bâtard-Montrachet 1996,
J-N Gagnard

Duck breast with honey and rosemary

Serves 6

2 large potatoes (Desiree or Maris Piper)
¾ cup butter
salt and pepper
6 duck breasts (Gressingham or Challans)
olive oil
1 ½ cups shelled lima beans
½ cup tomato fondue (page 81)
3 cups small mousserons des prés *(fairy ring mushrooms / Marasmius oreades)*
2–3 tablespoons clear honey
1 tablespoon white wine vinegar
1 ¼ cups duck or veal stock (page 264)
3 sprigs of rosemary

Cut the potatoes into ¾in thick slices, then trim into oval shapes. Put in a thick-bottomed pan with half the butter, a pinch of salt, and just enough water to cover. Place over high heat and cook until the water has completely evaporated and the potatoes touching the pan are golden brown. Remove from the heat and let rest for 15 minutes. Turn them over and set over high heat to color the other side, 2–3 minutes. Allow to rest in the fat.

Heat the oven to 400°F. Season the duck breasts and score the skin with a sharp knife. Place skin down in a smoking hot pan with a drop of olive oil. When well browned, turn over and place in the oven for 10 minutes. Remove from the pan and let rest in a warm place.

Blanch the lima beans in boiling salted water until just tender. Refresh in ice-cold water, drain, and then peel off the skins. Put the beans into a small saucepan with the tomato fondue to reheat gently.

Trim the mushrooms and, if necessary, wash very briefly. Pan fry in a little olive oil for a few seconds to release their liquid. Drain in a colander, then fry again until lightly crisp.

Into the pan in which you cooked the duck, put 1 ½ tablespoons of the honey and the vinegar and place over high heat. When caramelized, add the stock, and reduce to a light sauce consistency. Whisk in the remaining butter and a few leaves of chopped rosemary.

Brush the duck skins with the remaining honey and place under a hot broiler until crisp, about 2 minutes. Carve the duck and arrange on a bed of potato on warm serving plates. Spoon the vegetables and sauce around the potato.

If you are feeling extravagant, a slice of hot pan-fried foie gras on top of the duck finishes the dish off nicely.

Roast Bresse pigeon with fresh peas

Serves 6

6 Bresse pigeons (14oz–1lb each)
salt and pepper
olive oil
18 baby onions
1 large carrot
2½ cups shelled fresh peas
½ cup butter, cubed
9oz smoked bacon
1 cup chicken stock (page 264)
1 round lettuce, shredded

Bresse is a region in France near Lyon, famous for its poultry. The flavor and texture of these birds is quite unique and commands a high price. If you cannot find Bresse pigeons, make sure you choose the best quality young birds.

Heat the oven to 450°F. Season inside the pigeons, then smear the pigeons with olive oil and sprinkle with salt. Place in a hot roasting pan over high heat and brown the birds all over. Turn them on to their backs and roast in the oven for 12 minutes; the meat should be rosy pink. Remove from the oven, turn them breast side down so the juices permeate the breast meat, cover with tin foil and let rest in a warm place for 15 minutes before serving.

Peel and trim the baby onions. Peel and cut the carrot into 1¼in long batons. Cook the onions, carrot batons, and peas in boiling salted water until just tender. Refresh in ice-cold water and drain well. Cut the bacon into thin batons and blanch for 1 minute in boiling water; drain well.

Melt 1 tablespoon of butter in a wide saucepan. When it foams, add the bacon and cook until beginning to brown. Add the onions and cook for a further 3 minutes, rolling them around the pan from time to time. Then add the peas, carrots, and chicken stock and simmer for 10 minutes. Season well, then add the butter a little at a time, shaking the pan so the butter emulsifies and thickens the sauce. Just before serving, fold in the shredded lettuce leaves. Serve with the pigeons.

Roast black leg chicken with fresh pasta, foie gras, and truffles

Serves 4

1 black leg chicken (about 3lb)
olive oil
1 whole truffle (weighing
1–1½oz), thinly sliced
salt and pepper
⅔ cup butter, cubed
5 shallots, thickly sliced
⅓ cup fruity semi-sweet
white wine
1¼ cups chicken stock (page 264)
sherry vinegar
1lb fresh tagliatelle
7oz fresh foie gras
1oz truffle peelings,
chopped (or more!)
1 tablespoon truffle juice

Black leg chicken is a French breed; if you can't buy it you can substitute organic chicken.

Heat the oven to 400°F. Prepare the chicken for roasting by removing the wishbone, wing tips, and any giblets. Gently lift the skin from around the breast and thigh, using a little oil on your fingertips. Insert slices of truffle under the skin, then season the chicken inside and out and truss with kitchen string. Roast the chicken with oil and a little butter for 40 minutes, basting several times.

Remove from the oven and tip out any juices from the bird into the roasting pan. Remove the chicken from the pan, turn on to its breast, cover loosely with tin foil, and let rest in a warm place.

Spoon off excess fat from the roasting pan and replace with 1 tablespoon fresh butter. Sweat the shallots in the butter until translucent. Add the wine to deglaze the pan and boil to reduce by two-thirds. Add the chicken stock and reduce to a light sauce consistency. Whisk in the remaining butter, season, and add a couple of drops of sherry vinegar.

Meanwhile, cook the pasta in boiling salted water until al dente; drain well.

Cut the foie gras into small chunks approximately ½in square, then put them into a hot dry pan over medium heat for 15 seconds, so they begin to cook and render a little fat. Add the cooked pasta and turn gently until heated through. Season well and pour off a little of the fat. Add the chopped truffle and juice, turn up the heat for 15 seconds, then serve immediately, with the chicken.

Wine suggestion:
Sassicaia 'Tenuta San Guido' 1985,
Incisa della Rocchetta

Veal kidneys in a creamy three mustard sauce

Serves 4

2 whole veal kidneys
olive oil
salt and pepper
2 shallots, chopped
1 teaspoon butter
2 tablespoons brandy
¼ cup dry white wine
1 cup heavy cream
2 teaspoons wholegrain mustard
1 teaspoon Dijon mustard
1 teaspoon herb / tarragon mustard

To prepare the veal kidneys, carefully cut away the surrounding fat, then turn it upside down to reveal the fatty sinews. With the point of a sharp knife, cut around the sinews so the kidneys come away clean. Divide the kidneys into bite-sized morsels, following the natural lobes as much as possible.

Heat a thick-bottomed wide pan with a little olive oil until smoking hot. Add the kidneys and season lightly. Cook for 3–4 minutes (depending on size), turning the kidneys to seal all over. Tip into a colander to drain. The kidneys should still be very pink as they will finish cooking in the sauce.

In the same pan, sweat the shallots with the butter over medium heat for 5 minutes without letting them color, stirring frequently. Turn up the heat, add the brandy, and reduce by half. Add the wine and again reduce by half. Pour in the cream and reduce to a light sauce. Remove from the heat and whisk in all the mustard. Reheat gently—do not boil or it will become bitter—add the kidneys and heat through. Serve immediately with fresh brown tagliatelle.

Brown tagliatelle

1 ¾ cups wholewheat flour
½ cup bread flour
3 egg yolks
1 egg

Combine all the ingredients in a food processor, adding a few drops of water if needed; the dough should be pliable but not sticky. You can knead the dough by hand but this can be quite tough. Wrap and let rest in the refrigerator for 1 hour.

Roll out the pasta using a pasta machine, gradually bringing the setting down to 0. Cut into tagliatelle and hang over a broom handle to dry. The pasta can be kept on a tray, covered loosely with wax paper, for a week in a cool dry place.

To serve, cook in boiling salted water until al dente.

Braised shoulder of spring lamb

Serves 6

2 shoulders of baby lamb
olive oil
24 button onions
sea salt
3 garlic cloves, chopped
1 teaspoon cumin seeds
1 chili, cut in half lengthwise,
seeds removed
3 plum tomatoes, peeled, deseeded,
and chopped
⅓ cup Madeira
generous pinch of saffron strands
7fl oz fresh orange juice
2 cups chicken stock (page 264)

Heat the oven to 375°F. Take a flameproof casserole dish with plenty of room to hold the two shoulders laid flat, place over high heat, and add a generous amount of olive oil. Brown the lamb well on both sides.

Lower the heat to moderate and add the peeled button onions and a little sea salt; shake the pan from time to time so that the onions start to get a good color. After about 5 minutes add the garlic, cumin seeds, chili, and tomatoes, stir well and increase the heat to high. Pour in the Madeira and the saffron, and when they come to a boil add the orange juice and chicken stock. Bring back to a boil, then partially cover the pan, and place in the oven for 1 hour. Stir and turn the meat occasionally.

Let cool completely, then remove the lamb and place in the refrigerator for 1 hour.

Using a heavy knife or cleaver, cut the shoulders into three at the joints.

To serve: Reheat the meat in a non-stick pan with a little olive oil until caramelized. Remove the chili from the sauce, then reheat the sauce until piping hot. Pour the sauce over the meat and serve with couscous.

Wine suggestion:
Château Pichon-Lalande 1985
(Pauillac)

Brie stuffed with truffles

Serves 15–20

*1 Brie de Nangis (about 8in
diameter)*
6 truffles
salt and freshly ground pepper
1 tablespoon extra virgin olive oil
*1 tablespoon truffle juice
(optional)*

Use a Brie that is firm to the touch and not too ripe. You can use the larger Brie from Meaux or Melun, but should then increase the amount of truffles. Always try to purchase a Brie *fermier* and preferably *au lait cru* (made from unpasteurized milk), as the taste is far superior to that of pasteurized cheese.

Fresh Perigord truffles are best for this recipe as the intensity of flavor will permeate the Brie more effectively. However, you can substitute canned truffles; a 7oz can will be enough for this recipe.

Cut the Brie in half horizontally with a long thin knife. Slice the truffles thinly and season with salt, pepper, olive oil, and truffle juice if you have any. Spread the truffles evenly over the bottom half of the Brie, replace the top half and wrap it in its original paper. Push back into its box and refrigerate for two to three days to mature.

To serve: Remove from the refrigerator at least an hour before serving, with toasted pain de campagne and mâche (lamb's lettuce/corn salad) seasoned with red wine vinegar and olive oil. In the restaurant we serve this as a cheese course, but at home I'll serve extra salad and have it as light meal in itself.

Wine suggestion:
Vieux Château Certan 1985 (Pomerol)

Almond floating islands

Serves 6–8

1 quart milk

1 vanilla bean, split

12 egg yolks

3½ cups caster sugar

almond extract

1¼ cups slivered almonds

about 1 quart each milk and water

8 egg whites

Begin by making a crème anglaise. Bring the milk and vanilla bean to a boil, remove from the heat, cover, and let infuse for 10 minutes. Beat the egg yolks with $1^1/_4$ cups of the sugar until thick and creamy. Bring the milk back to a boil and pour on to the yolk mixture, whisking continuously. Return the mixture to the saucepan and cook over low heat, stirring continuously with a rubber spatula, until the custard thickens slightly. Add a few drops of almond extract to give a delicate flavor. Pour into a serving dish and keep cold.

Toast the slivered almonds under a medium-low broiler, turning a couple of times until lightly and evenly browned.

Pour equal quantities of milk and water into a wide pan to give a depth of 2½in. Add about 3 tablespoons of the sugar— just enough to sweeten—and bring to simmering.

Whisk the egg whites until frothy, then add a scant 1¼ cups of sugar and continue to whisk until firm but not too stiff. Using a tablespoon and palette knife dipped in cold water, shape the egg whites into six large quenelles. Gently lower the quenelles into the simmering liquid, rinsing the spoon in cold water each time. Simmer for 2 minutes, then flip over and simmer for another 2 minutes. Remove with a slotted spoon and place on a wire rack with a tray beneath.

To assemble: Place the meringue 'islands' on the crème anglaise and sprinkle with the toasted almonds. Put the remaining sugar into a thick-bottomed saucepan over low heat until dissolved, then turn the heat to high to caramelize. Dip the pan in cold water for a few seconds to halt the cooking, then pour the caramel over the islands. Serve within 2 hours, otherwise the caramel will lose its crunchiness. Do not refrigerate, as this hastens the softening of the caramel.

Pink praline tart

Serves 6

½lb sweet pastry dough
(page 279)
2 cups pink pralines
7fl oz heavy cream

Pink pralines (*pralines roses*) are a speciality of the Lyonnais region of France and are found in every food shop around Lyon. They are basically sugar-coated vanilla-flavored almonds colored with red food coloring. This tart can be made with ordinary sugared almonds, but *pralines roses* give it a very attractive red color when cooked. I love this very sweet, sticky dessert, even though I do not have a sweet tooth.

Heat the oven to 350°F. Roll out the pastry and use to line a buttered tart pan (8in diameter x 1in deep). Line the pastry dough with wax paper and dried beans and cook for 15 minutes, then remove the beans and paper and cook for a further 5 minutes, until the bottom of the tart is dry and just beginning to turn pale brown.

Crush the pralines with a rolling pin until they are the size of small gravel, mix with the cream and then pour into the pastry shell. Cook for about 15 minutes, until the mixture bubbles and turns a rich red-brown color. Let cool before serving.

Have we ever inspired the surreal humour of Spike Milligan? Or did we just give him food for thought?

Rhubarb compote with kirsch sabayon and strawberry cordial, pepper tuiles

Serves 8

8 rhubarb stalks

2 cups sweet white wine (e.g.,

Sauternes)

⅔ cup caster sugar

2 vanilla beans, split

Rhubarb compote

Wash the rhubarb, cut off the leaves, then slice the rhubarb into 1½in sticks. Bring the wine to a boil with the sugar and vanilla beans, add the rhubarb, and partially cover with a lid. Simmer until the rhubarb is soft yet still holds its shape: 3–5 minutes, depending on the thickness of the rhubarb. Remove from the heat, let cool, then drain in a colander, saving the juice for a refreshing cordial drink.

Pepper tuiles

⅔ cup unsalted butter, softened
1 ¼ cups caster sugar
7 fl oz canned coconut milk
1 teaspoon cracked black pepper
1 teaspoon cracked Sichuan pepper
3½ oz all-purpose flour

Mix the butter, sugar, and coconut milk with a whisk. When smooth, add the peppers and fold in the flour. Let rest in the refrigerator for at least 1 hour.

Heat the oven to 350°F. Spread the mixture very thinly on a non-stick baking sheet and cook until light golden. While still warm, cut into circles with a pastry dough cutter and let cool on a sheet of wax paper. The tuiles can be stored for several days in an airtight container.

Kirsch sabayon

1 egg
1 egg yolk
¼ cup caster sugar
1 sheet of gelatin
⅓ cup kirsch
1 ¼ cups whipping cream

Whisk the egg, yolk, and sugar for 10 minutes until frothy. Meanwhile, soak the gelatin in cold water until soft, then squeeze dry and melt in a little of the kirsch. Whisk the gelatin into the egg mixture together with the rest of the warmed, but not boiled, kirsch. Whisk for a further minute, then fold in the lightly whipped cream. Let set in the refrigerator.

Strawberry cordial

2 cups strawberries
½ cup caster sugar

Hull the strawberries, cut in half lengthwise and mix with the sugar in a small bowl. The amount of sugar you need will depend on the sweetness of the fruit. Cover tightly with cling film and set over a double boiler for 5 minutes. Let cool, then strain through a cheesecloth-lined sieve and refrigerate. (The strained strawberries are great in yoghurt for breakfast; the cordial is delicious in a champagne cocktail).

To assemble: Place a ring mold (1½in diameter x ¾in deep) in the middle of a soup plate. Pack with rhubarb. Using a hot spoon, put a quenelle of sabayon on top of the compote, pour some strawberry cordial around, and finish with a pepper tuile pushed into the sabayon.

Wine suggestion:
Coteaux du Layon 'Clos des Bonnes Blanches' 1996, V Ogereau

Rich chocolate truffle with two sauces

Serves 12

2¼lb unsweetened chocolate
(78% cocoa solids), chopped

1 quart whipping cream

Melt the chocolate in a double boiler. Whisk the cream in a large bowl until it leaves a light ribbon trail when the whisk is lifted. Pour the melted chocolate into the cream, whisking all the time until well incorporated.

Line a stainless steel mold (8in x 12in x 1½in) with chocolate sponge cake and sprinkle with sugar syrup to moisten lightly. Spread the truffle mixture over the sponge with a palette knife, then refrigerate for at least 6 hours.

Chocolate sponge

6 tablespoons all-purpose flour

2 tablespoons unsweetened cocoa
powder

¾ cup ground almonds

1 tablespoon unsalted butter

½oz dark chocolate

½ cup caster sugar

1 egg

2 large egg yolks

3 egg whites

Heat the oven to 350°F. Butter and flour two baking sheets (8in x 12in). Sift the flour and cocoa powder together, then stir in the ground almonds. Melt the butter and chocolate together in a small bowl.

Beat 2½oz of the sugar with the whole egg and 2 yolks until thick and foamy. Beat the egg whites with the remaining sugar until stiff. Fold the whites into the yolk mixture, then fold in the flour, cocoa, and almonds, and finally fold in the butter and chocolate. Spread on the prepared baking sheet and cook for 10 minutes. Invert on to a wire rack and let cool.

Sugar syrup

½ cup caster sugar

7 tablespoons water

Put the sugar and water in a small saucepan over low heat and stir gently to dissolve the sugar. When completely dissolved, bring to a boil for 1–2 minutes. Let cool.

Chocolate decorations

Melt 5–7oz dark chocolate over low heat. Drizzle on to a baking sheet lined with wax paper, to form decorative swirls. Let set in the refrigerator.

Sweet fresh mint sauce

2 cups milk
6 egg yolks
½ cup caster sugar
¼lb fresh mint leaves, chopped
peppermint liqueur

Bring the milk to a boil. Beat the egg yolks with the sugar until thick and creamy. Pour the hot milk on to the yolk mixture, whisking continuously. Pour the mixture back into the saucepan and cook over low heat, stirring continuously with a rubber spatula, until the custard thickens slightly; do not let it boil. While still hot, add the mint leaves. Cover and let steep until cool.

Pass the sauce through a fine sieve and chill. Finally, whisk in a few drops of peppermint liqueur.

Ginger sauce

2 cups milk
6 egg yolks
½ cup caster sugar
2 tablespoons ginger confit and
syrup (page 62)

Bring the milk to a boil. Beat the egg yolks with the sugar until thick and creamy. Pour the hot milk on to the yolk mixture, whisking continuously. Pour the mixture back into the saucepan and cook over low heat, stirring continuously with a rubber spatula, until the custard thickens slightly; do not let it boil. Pass through a fine sieve and leave until cold.

Stir in the ginger confit and 2 tablespoons of the ginger syrup for a subtle ginger flavor.

To serve: Cut the truffle cake into small rectangles. Decorate with the chocolate swirls and surround with a generous spoonful of each of the two sauces.

Delice glacé au Tokaji

Serves 12

54 prunes, pitted
1 ⅔ cups Tokaji Aszu
8 egg yolks
⅔ cup caster sugar
2 tablespoons water
2 cups heavy cream

Begin a week ahead by putting the prunes in a bowl and adding enough Tokaji to cover (about 1 cup).

Prepare the dessert the day before you want to serve it. Put the egg yolks in a large bowl. Put the sugar and water in a small saucepan over low heat and slowly bring to a boil. Boil until the temperature reaches 260°F on a sugar thermometer, then immediately pour on to the yolks and whisk until very pale, thick, and creamy. Let cool.

Lightly whip the cream and fold into the yolk mixture, with ⅔ cup Tokaji. Chop six of the prunes and add to the mixture. Pour into 12 ramekins, cover, and freeze for 24 hours.

To serve: Blend 12 prunes with a little of their marinade to make a thin sauce. Turn out the Tokaji mousse on to serving plates. Drizzle the sauce around the mousse, and serve with three marinated prunes and a honey tuile (page 49).

In the restaurant, we pipe the tuile mixture to make a crisp cage to contain the delice

Wine suggestion:
Tokaji Aszu Birsalma's 5 Puttonyos 1991, Royal Tokaji Wine Company

*Artichokes Baby carrot.
Dandelion Fennel Fr.
Melons Peaches Radi
Tom.*

Summer

Baby turnips Cherries Crab
nage blanc Lettuce Mackerel
es Raspberries Strawberries
oes Wild arugula Zucchini

Chilled mushroom soup with tapenade

Serves 4

2 cups mixed fresh mushrooms
3 tablespoons butter
juice of 1 lemon
2 cups chicken stock (page 264)
½ cup heavy cream
1 tablespoon tapenade (page 45)
salt, pepper, cayenne pepper
fresh basil and chervil

Clean the mushrooms and cut into chunks. Cook with the butter over low heat for 5 minutes. Add the lemon juice and stock, turn up the heat, and boil for a further 5 minutes.

Purée in a blender until completely smooth. Pour into a bowl, cover, and chill for at least 1 hour.

Whisk the cream until it forms soft peaks, then fold in the tapenade. Fold this mixture into the mushroom soup, and season to taste with salt, pepper, and cayenne pepper. Sprinkle with the freshly chopped herbs just before serving.

Grilled mackerel on iced tomato soup

Serves 8

The mackerel must be as fresh as possible, firm and shiny.

4 mackerel fillets
4 very ripe plum tomatoes
4 very ripe beef tomatoes
juice of 1 orange
8 cilantro seeds
salt and pepper
1 tablespoon tomato paste
1 tablespoon sherry vinegar
1 cucumber
olive oil
lemon juice

Blanch the tomatoes in boiling water for 15 seconds, then refresh in ice-cold water. Peel off the skins and cut in half; squeeze out the seeds, then chop roughly. Put the tomato flesh into a blender with the orange juice, cilantro seeds, salt, pepper and tomato paste, blend until smooth, and then press through a fine sieve. Check for seasoning and add a little sherry vinegar to sharpen the taste. Chill for at least 3 hours. The air bubbles will come out of the tomato soup and the color will intensify to deep red.

Peel the cucumber and remove the seeds. Cut the flesh into thin julienne strips, 2in long. Season with salt, pepper, olive oil, and lemon juice.

Using a pair of tweezers, remove the pin bones from the fish, then wash and pat dry. Cut each fillet into two diamonds, brush with a very small amount of olive oil, and season with salt and pepper. Cook under a hot broiler.

Place the cucumber in a neat pile in the center of the soup plates. Add the hot mackerel, pour the cold tomato soup around, and decorate with deep-fried basil leaves.

Wine suggestion:
Bellet, Domaine de la Source 1998,
J Dalmasso

107

Smoked eel and carrot salad

Serves 6

2–3 carrots

salt and pepper

1 teaspoon light brown sugar

1 smoked eel (2½lb)

3 tablespoons peanut oil

2 sprigs of fresh cilantro

Peel the carrots and cut into a very fine julienne, season with salt and pepper, stir in the sugar, cover with plastic wrap, and refrigerate for 12 hours.

If the eel has not been skinned or filleted this is not such a daunting task as it may seem—certainly not as difficult as skinning live eels. Simply score the skin near the head and pull the skin toward the tail; it comes off as easily as peeling a banana! To fillet, use a thin-bladed knife and follow the backbone all the way down to the tail.

Cut the eel fillets into neat diamond shapes (¾in wide) and set aside.

Take the carrots out of the refrigerator; they will have given off a golden colored liquid. Drain the carrots, reserving the liquid. Press the carrots into a ring (2¼in diameter x 1½in deep), then remove the ring and arrange the eel diamonds on top. Add a spoonful of horseradish cream. Blend the cilantro leaves with the oil with a hand blender or mortar and pestle. Drizzle the cilantro oil and the carrot juices on the plates to give a bright, vibrant, summer salad.

Horseradish cream

3 tablespoons heavy cream

2 tablespoons horseradish relish

1 spring onion, thinly sliced

Whip the cream until stiff. Stir in the horseradish relish and scallion and chill in the refrigerator until ready to serve.

Wine suggestion:
Alsace Gewurztraminer 1997, Hugel

Chilled lobster consommé scented with marjoram and celery

Serves 8

1 celery stalk, finely chopped

1 shallot, finely chopped

1 small carrot, finely chopped

2 sprigs of marjoram

6oz minced lean beef or chicken

3 egg whites

3 quarts lobster stock (page 267)

7fl oz sweet Madeira

sea salt

1 teaspoon cracked white pepper

This is a refreshing summer soup, slightly set and sweetly scented with marjoram.

Mix the celery, shallot, carrot, marjoram leaves, minced beef or chicken, and egg whites; whisk until the egg whites have started to froth. Gently mix this into the cold stock and Madeira in a thick-bottomed saucepan. Bring to a boil, stirring gently with a wooden spatula and scraping the bottom of the pan. As soon as the liquid starts to bubble, turn down the heat so it barely simmers and stop stirring. A crust of egg white will form on the surface; make a hole in the center of this to allow the stock to clarify properly. Simmer very gently for 20 minutes, then remove from the heat and check the seasoning. Using a ladle, gently pass the liquid through a cheesecloth-lined strainer that has the cracked peppercorns in it. Chill for at least 2 hours, or overnight.

Serve in soup plates, garnished with small pieces of lobster, a few marjoram leaves, and tender celery heart leaves.

Spicy pigeon and lobster salad

Serves 4

1 cooked lobster (about 1lb 6oz)

1 tablespoon red wine vinegar

1 tablespoon herb mustard

5 tablespoons extra virgin olive oil

salt and pepper

1 large pigeon (about 1lb 2oz)

1 cinnamon stick

4 cloves

1 red chili

1 tablespoon Chinese
5-spice powder

1 tablespoon sugar

2 teaspoons sherry vinegar

1 quart chicken stock (page 264)

2 shallots, finely chopped

1 teaspoon hazelnut oil

curly endive/frisée lettuce and
radicchio, cut into thin strips

Crack the lobster and scape all the coral out of the head cavity. Pass this through a fine sieve into a small bowl and make a lobster vinaigrette by whisking the red wine vinegar, herb mustard, extra virgin olive oil, salt, and pepper.

Heat the oven to 450°F. Season inside the pigeon, smear the outside with olive oil, and sprinkle with salt. Place in a hot roasting pan over high heat and brown all over. Turn on to its back and roast in the oven for 12 minutes; the meat should be rosy pink. Remove from the oven, turn breast side down so the juices permeate the breast meat, cover with tin foil and let rest in a warm place for 10 minutes. Remove the meat from the bones; roughly chop the bones.

Heat the spices in a saucepan to release the aromas. Add the sugar, sherry vinegar, chopped pigeon bones, and chicken stock, bring to a boil and skim; simmer for 15 minutes. Pass through a cheesecloth-lined colander or fine sieve into a clean pan and reduce until syrupy. Remove from the heat and add the shallots, then whisk in the hazelnut oil to emulsify.

Dress the curly endive and radicchio with the lobster vinaigrette. Thinly slice the pigeon and lobster, arrange around the salad, and pour a little of the spicy sauce over the pigeon and lobster. Garnish with thin croûtons of fried baguette and a fine julienne of raw celery.

Spicy fresh crab salad

Serves 6

1lb 6oz white crab meat
1 large avocado, diced
2 scallions, sliced thinly
juice of 2 limes
1 tablespoon sesame oil
salt
Tabasco sauce
7oz brown crab meat, pushed through a fine sieve
watercress, to garnish

Wine suggestion:
Domaine de la Rectorie 'L'argile' 1997
(Vin de pays de la Côte Vermeille)

3 plum tomatoes, peeled, deseeded and chopped
pinch of sugar
1 teaspoon tomato paste
7fl oz whipping cream
1 tablespoon green peppercorns in brine, lightly crushed

Crab is my favorite seafood; I think all the work involved in picking the meat out of it makes it taste all the better. Besides which, the depth of flavor is superb, whether you are using small soft-shell crabs deep-fried in tempura batter or little velvet crabs to make soup. The cock crab is larger and therefore has more meat, but some say the female crabs are sweeter, especially the brown meat.

The best way to cook a crab is to drown it first: Just submerge it in cold fresh water for 5 minutes and it will gently pass away. Then cook it in boiling salted water for 18 minutes (for a large, 4½lb crab). If all this together with the cracking and picking seems like too much work, buy the best quality fresh picked claw meat—not frozen or pasteurized.

Put the white crab meat in a bowl and add the avocado, scallions, lime juice, sesame oil, salt, and Tabasco. Mix gently with a fork; do not overmix as you should keep the delicate flaky texture of the crab meat.

Place a spoonful of the brown meat in each serving dish, then add the white meat mixture. Top with a small quenelle of peppered tomato mousse; shape the quenelle by dipping 2 dessertspoons into hot water. Garnish with watercress.

Peppered tomato mousse

Put the chopped tomatoes and a pinch of sugar in a saucepan over low heat, stirring occasionally until all the moisture has evaporated and the tomatoes are thick. Let cool.

Add the tomato paste and pass through a fine sieve. Whip the cream until firm but not too stiff, then fold in the tomato mixture and the green peppercorns. Chill in the refrigerator until firm.

Stuffed duck necks with pistachios and raw baby vegetable salad

Serves 10–12

3 long duck necks

1 quart veal stock (page 264)

¾lb fresh foie gras

salt and pepper

brandy

1½lb plump duck breasts (magrets de canard)

¼lb pork back fat

1 teaspoon crushed cilantro seeds

2 teaspoons fresh thyme leaves

¾ cup shelled pistachio nuts

3 sprigs of thyme

Cooking pâté in a duck neck is commonly done in the southwest of France. The stuffing varies from one recipe to another but this is one that I am particularly fond of. Great as a summer appetizer or for a picnic.

Ask for duck necks from large ducks, probably Barbary or Aylesbury, so that when you have removed the neck, head, and windpipe you are left with a tube about 8–9in long. Make sure there are no incisions in the skin.

Boil the veal stock until it reduces down to 4 tablespoons of sticky glaze (*glace de viande*). Keep the glaze at room temperature, otherwise it will set firm.

Cut the foie gras into chunks about ½in square. Season lightly with salt and pepper, sprinkle with brandy, cover, and refrigerate.

Trim the duck breasts thoroughly, removing all fat and sinew. Cut the duck meat into ¼in dice and place in a bowl. Remove the rind from the pork, cut the pork into small dice, and add to the duck. Add the crushed cilantro seeds, thyme leaves, and veal glaze, sprinkle with more brandy, and season well with salt and pepper. Finely mince a quarter of this mixture, then beat this back into the diced mixture. Fold in the foie gras and pistachios, taking care not to break up the foie gras.

Tie one end of each neck securely with string. Push the forcemeat into the duck necks, tie the other end and several times along the neck to help keep its shape. Put in a large saucepan and cover with well salted cold water. Add the sprigs of thyme and bring the water up to 160°F. Begin timing from the moment it reaches that temperature; after 40 minutes, remove from the heat and leave the duck necks in the water until tepid. Remove from the water, cover, and refrigerate for at least 12 hours.

To serve, slice the duck necks at an angle and serve with baby vegetable salad.

Baby vegetable salad

Clean, peel, and trim radishes, baby carrots, turnips, fennel, and celery hearts. Using a mandolin, slice the vegetables as thinly as possible. Dress with a little extra virgin olive oil, sea salt, pepper, and a few drops of red wine vinegar.

Rabbit terrine cooked in Chablis with grain mustard

Serves 8

1 rabbit (domestic, not wild, about
3½lb)
2 tablespoons olive oil
1 carrot, diced
1 onion, diced
4 strips smoked bacon, diced
1¾ cups Chablis wine
½ calf's foot, split in two
2 bay leaves
1 sprig of thyme
1 quart chicken stock (page 264)
salt and pepper
2 tablespoons grain mustard
generous amount of flat-leaf
parsley, tarragon, and chervil,
roughly chopped

Prepare the rabbit by removing the heart and lungs, but if you like the liver and kidneys you can leave them in to cook with the rabbit.

Heat the oil in a large casserole dish and seal the rabbit on all sides. Add the carrot, onion, and bacon and cook over medium heat until lightly colored. Add the wine and boil for 1 minute, then add the calf's foot, bay leaves, thyme, and stock. Bring to a boil, cover with a lid, and cook in a very low oven at 250°F for 1½ hours.

Take out of the oven and let cool. When hand hot, pick all the meat off the bones and shred between your fingers into a mixing bowl.

Pass the cooking liquid through a colander into a saucepan. Return the carrot and onion to the meat. Boil the cooking liquid and skim thoroughly to remove as much fat and scum as possible; reduce by one-third and pour on to the meat. Stir in the mustard and herbs, check for seasoning, and then pour into a porcelain terrine; refrigerate for at least 12 hours.

Serve with toasted sourdough bread, and a little salad of chives, chervil, tarragon, watercress, wild arugula and dandelion dressed in red wine vinegar and a rich olive oil.

Wine suggestion:
Chablis 'Montée de Tonnerre' 1998,
Durup

Marinated salmon with crushed potatoes and caviar

Makes 50–60 slices

1 wild or organic salmon (11lb)
3 tablespoons cracked black pepper
3 tablespoons cracked white pepper
1 tablespoon cracked cilantro seeds
6 cloves, broken up
2 star anise pods, broken up
2¼ cups coarse sea salt
1½ cups caster sugar
grated zest and juice of 1 lime
grated zest and juice of 1 lemon
1 big bunch of dill, chopped
oscietre caviar (allow 1 tablespoon per person—or more)

Fillet the salmon, remove the pin bones, and lightly score the skin; rinse under cold water and pat dry.

Crush the spices together in a blender but do not grind to a dust. Mix the spices with the salt, sugar, zest, and juice. Spread some of this mixture on a long stainless steel tray and lay a side of salmon on top, skin side down. Cover with some dill and spice mixture, then lay the other fillet on top, nose to tail and skin side up. Cover with the remaining spice mixture, then a piece of plastic wrap, and press down. Weigh down with about 7lb of weights, and refrigerate for 36 hours.

Drain off the liquid and turn the two fillets over, press again, and refrigerate for a further 12–24 hours, depending how strongly you want the fish to taste of the marinade.

Remove from the marinade and dry the fish with a cloth. Brush the flesh with a little English mustard and sprinkle with dry dill. Wrap in plastic wrap and refrigerate until needed.

To serve: Bake 1 large potato for 4 people, scoop out the flesh and crush with a fork, season with salt and pepper, moisten with a little butter, and add a sliced scallion. Place a ring mold (1½in diameter x ¼in deep) in the center of a plate and fill with the warm potato. Arrange several thin slices of marinated salmon around the potato and top the potato with as much caviar as you wish. Finish with a quenelle of horseradish cream and serve with hot brioche toast.

Horseradish cream
Lightly whip 1 cup of whipping cream; fold in 2 tablespoons horseradish relish, 1 teaspoon mustard, and a pinch of salt.

Paris mushroom bavarois

Serves 10–12

2½ cups white button mushrooms,
thinly sliced
salt, white pepper, and nutmeg
3⅓ cups whipping cream
3 sheets of gelatin
lemon juice

Put the mushrooms in a saucepan, season well, add half the cream, and bring to a boil; the mushrooms will be cooked in 2 minutes. Soak the gelatin in cold water until soft, squeeze dry, and add to the mushrooms; purée in a blender until smooth. Let cool.

When nearly set, fold in the remaining cream, lightly whipped, check the seasoning, and add a little lemon juice if needed. Cover and refrigerate for at least 6 hours.

Using two tablespoons dipped in hot water, shape into quenelles and serve with toasted brioche.

Variation: Line individual ramekins with sliced cooked mushrooms and aspic made with mushroom-scented veal stock. Fill with the bavarois and refrigerate. Invert to serve.

When Charlie Chaplin visited Le Gavroche he enjoyed it so much he booked again the following two nights. More than a decade later, Robert Redford managed to find Chaplin's signature in the visitors' book

Grilled red mullet on pea and tomato risotto

Serves 4

4 fillets of red mullet (5oz each)
½ cup heavy cream
1 cup frozen petits pois
salt and pepper
½ onion, chopped
butter
1 cup arborio rice
⅔ cup dry white wine
2 cups chicken stock (page 264)
1 cup cooked fresh peas
2 tablespoons Parmesan, grated
olive oil
16 dried tomato halves
(page 273), diced
balsamic vinegar
2 sprigs of tarragon

Rinse the red mullet, dry with paper towel, and remove the pin bones using a pair of tweezers.

Boil the heavy cream and add the frozen petits pois, season with salt and pepper, and then blend until smooth; set aside for later use.

Sweat the onion in a little butter, without letting it color. When tender, add the rice and cook for a few minutes, stirring continuously. When the rice is shiny, pour on the wine and cook, still stirring, until fully absorbed. Start adding the hot chicken stock a ladleful at a time, and reduce the heat to a simmer. Continue adding the hot stock a little at a time, stirring occasionally, until all the stock is absorbed; the risotto should be rich and creamy, yet the grains of rice should still have a slight bite. To finish the risotto, stir in the fresh peas, grated Parmesan, and a tablespoon of butter, then the pea purée and season with salt and pepper.

Warm the tomatoes with a little olive oil and balsamic vinegar and the tarragon leaves. Season the red mullet, brush with olive oil, and broil until cooked and the skin has bubbled.

Serve the risotto on warmed plates with the tomatoes around the outside. Place the mullet on top of the risotto and serve immediately.

Wine suggestion:
Domaine Gauby 1998
(Vin de pays des Côtes Catalanes)

Sole in a creamy carrot velouté sauce

Serves 4

4 small Dover soles (1lb each)
6 large carrots
1 tablespoon butter
2 shallots, finely chopped
⅓ cup dry white vermouth or
Noilly Prat
⅓ cup dry white wine
salt and pepper
1 cup crème fraîche
juice of 1 lemon

Skin the soles and use a pair of heavy-duty scissors to cut off the head, tail, and small bones around the edge of the fish. Heat the oven to 350°F.

Peel the carrots and julienne five of them; set aside. Chop the trimmings and cut the remaining carrot into small dice. Blanch in salted boiling water until well done, drain, and press through a fine sieve.

Lightly butter an ovenproof dish large enough to take the soles; sprinkle the fish with the chopped shallots and carrot julienne. Pour on the wine and vermouth and bring to a boil. Season with salt and pepper, cover with buttered wax paper, and put in the oven for 6 minutes, then turn over and cook for a further 6 minutes.

Take the soles out and put on warm plates or a serving dish, with twirls of the julienne carrots. Keep warm.

Pour the cooking liquid into a saucepan and bring to a boil, add the crème fraîche and lemon juice, and check the seasoning. Finally, thicken the sauce with the carrot purée. Serve with spinach puff pastry turnovers.

Spinach puff pastry turnover

3½oz puff pastry (page 278)
⅔ cup creamed spinach
(page 179)
1 egg yolk, beaten with a little
water and a pinch of salt

Roll out the pastry on a lightly floured surface to a thickness of ⅛in. Using a fluted cutter (2¼in diameter), cut out four circles and place in the refrigerator to firm up and rest for 20 minutes.

Heat the oven to 400°F. Put a heaping teaspoon of the cold spinach in the center of each pastry circle, then brush around the edge of the pastry with beaten egg. Fold the pastry over to form half circles and pinch the edges to seal. Brush the top with beaten egg and score lightly in a lattice pattern, then place in the hot oven for 9 minutes, until puffed and golden brown. Serve hot.

Singer Gilbert O'Sullivan had a string of hit songs in the 1970s

123

Stuffed sea bass with fennel

Serves 2

1 sea bass (2¼lb)
2–3 large fennel bulbs
½ onion, finely chopped
olive oil
¾ cup heavy cream
1 tablespoon pastis (e.g., Ricard)
1 teaspoon cornflour
6 baby new season onions (grelot onions—the type that look like bulbous scallions)
olive oil
2 sprigs of thyme
1 bay leaf
salt and pepper
⅔ cup dry white wine
½ cup water
6 dried tomatoes (page 273)

Scale the fish and remove the eyes and gills. Snip off the fins with a pair of heavy-duty scissors. Using a filleting knife, slit the fish along the backbone and remove the bones and guts, taking care not to pierce the belly. Remove the pin bones with a pair of tweezers, rinse in cold water, and dry.

Finely chop half of the fennel. Sweat the onion with the olive oil for 5 minutes. Add the fennel and cook for a further 3–4 minutes, stirring occasionally, until nearly tender. Pour in the cream, turn up the heat, and reduce until it starts to thicken. Mix the pastis with the cornflour until smooth. Pour into a boiling fennel mixture and whisk well for 15 seconds, then remove from the heat. Season well and set aside.

Slice the remaining fennel lengthwise into ¼in slices. Peel the baby onions and, if bigger than a marble, cut into halves or quarters. Cook the onions and fennel with a few drops of olive oil in a smoking hot, wide, thick-bottomed pan. Cook until well browned, turning occasionally, then add the thyme and bay leaf and season well. Add the wine and bring to a boil, then add the water, and turn the heat down. Cover with wax paper and simmer gently for about 12 minutes, until the vegetables are tender but still a little crunchy. To finish, add the dried tomatoes and a swirl of extra virgin olive oil. Bring to the table in the pan.

Heat the oven to 400°F and place a baking sheet into the oven to heat up. Place the fish on a large sheet of lightly oiled wax paper. Season with salt and pepper and fill with the creamed fennel stuffing, then fold the paper around the fish to form a long parcel; twist the ends together to seal. Place the parcel on the hot baking sheet and cook for 8 minutes. Turn the fish over and cook for a further 7 minutes. Serve in the parcel and open at table to release the aromas.

Wine suggestion:
Chardonnay 'Tête de Cuvée' 1998, Domaine du Tariquet (Vin de pays des Côtes de Gascogne)

Monkfish basquaise

Serves 6

2 red, 2 green, and 2 yellow bell
peppers
4 ripe plum tomatoes
6 pieces of monkfish (5–6oz each)
6 slices of Bayonne or Parma ham
olive oil
2 garlic cloves, chopped
1 teaspoon tomato paste
2 sprigs of thyme
1–2 chilies
1 bay leaf
3 tablespoons water
salt and pepper
2 red onions, thinly sliced

Put the peppers under a hot broiler until the skins are burned and blistered all over. Remove from the heat, cover with plastic wrap, and let cool. When cold, remove the skins, stalks, and seeds and cut into long strips.

Blanch the tomatoes in boiling water for 15 seconds, then refresh in ice-cold water. Peel off the skins and cut in half; squeeze out the seeds, then chop roughly.

Heat the oven 425°F. Wrap each piece of monkfish in a slice of ham, securing the ham with wooden toothpicks. Seal over high heat in a roasting pan with a little olive oil, then place in the oven for 7–8 minutes.

Remove the fish from the roasting pan and keep warm. Add the garlic to the pan and cook for 1 minute, then add the tomato paste, thyme, chilies, bay leaf, water, and chopped tomatoes and simmer over low heat for 6 minutes. Season with salt and add any juices that have run out of the fish.

Put a drop of olive oil in a non-stick frying pan and cook the onions until tender and lightly colored, then add the peppers, season with salt and pepper, and reheat for 1 minute.

Cut each piece of monkfish in half and serve on a spoonful of the tomato sauce. Spoon some of the onion and pepper mixture on top and serve hot.

Wine suggestion:
Range du Béarn 1998, Domaine Nigri

Black bream cooked in its marinade

Serves 6

6 fillets of black bream
(4–5½oz each)
1 carrot
1 onion
1 fennel bulb
½ cup dry white wine
¼ cup water
1 tablespoon white wine vinegar
juice of ½ orange and ½ lemon
1 teaspoon demerara sugar
½ teaspoon cumin seeds
sea salt and coarsely ground
pepper
3 tablespoons strong, fragrant
olive oil
small sprigs of flat-leaf parsley

Black bream is sometimes regarded as a lesser fish than the gilt-head bream (daurade royale), yet when fresh and cooked in this way it is truly delicious.

Rinse the fish, dry with paper towels, and remove the pin bones using a pair of tweezers.

Peel the onion, carrot, and fennel. Slice the onion into thin rings. Make five cuts down the length of the carrot with a cannelle knife, then slice the carrot into thin flower-shaped rounds. Slice the fennel thinly lengthwise.

Put the wine, water, vinegar, fruit juices, sugar, and cumin seeds in a saucepan, bring to a boil, and season with a little sea salt and pepper. Add the vegetables, stir, and remove from the heat; cover and let cool completely.

Lay the fish flat in an ovenproof glass or earthware dish. Pour on the cold marinade and the olive oil, cover, and refrigerate for 6–12 hours.

Heat the oven to 375°F. Scatter the parsley over the fish, cover with wax paper and cook for 12 minutes; it should be somewhat undercooked and just warm.

Roast gilt-head bream with citrus fruit vinaigrette

Serves 4

4 gilt-head bream
(14oz–1lb 2oz each)
1 orange
1 lemon
1 pink grapefruit
salt and pepper
2 shallots, finely chopped
4 tablespoons extra virgin olive oil
2 sprigs of basil

Heat the oven to 425°F. Scale the fish and remove the eyes and gills. Slit the belly and remove the guts. Rinse well under cold running water and pat dry.

Peel the fruit and segment, removing all the pith, holding the fruit over a bowl to collect the juices. Squeeze the remaining central part of the fruits to extract all the juice.

Slash the skin of the fish three times on each side, and season with salt and pepper. Cook in a non-stick ovenproof pan with a drop of olive oil over a fierce heat so as to crisp the skin, turning the fish after 3 minutes. When both sides are browned, place in the oven for about 5 minutes, depending on size.

Take the fish out of the pan and place them on plates or a serving dish to keep warm. Put the shallots in the same pan with 1 tablespoon of the olive oil and cook briskly for 1 minute. Add the fruit juices and reduce by one-third; pour in any juices from the fish. Add the fruit segments and the remaining olive oil, then immediately remove from the heat and pour over the fish. Sprinkle with the shredded basil leaves and serve; this should be warm, not hot.

Wine suggestion:
Côtes de Provence Cuvée Clarendon
1996, Domaine Gavoty

Roast turbot with grain mustard and tomatoes

Serves 6

6 thick pieces of turbot
(5–6oz each)
salt and pepper
1 tablespoon olive oil
3 shallots, chopped
2 tablespoons dry white wine
1 tablespoon Dijon grain mustard
2 tablespoons coarsely
chopped parsley
6 plum tomatoes, peeled, deseeded
and diced

Heat a large non-stick frying pan until very hot. Add the olive oil and cook the lightly seasoned turbot over high heat for about 2 minutes, then turn and cook the other side for a further 2–3 minutes. Remove from the pan, cover with wax paper, and keep warm; any juices that come out of the fish can be poured into the sauce.

With the pan still on high heat, add the shallots and cook for 30 seconds, stirring so they don't burn, then pour in the wine and reduce by half. Whisk in the beurre blanc and the remaining ingredients; do not allow to boil.

Serve the fish on a bed of baby spinach, cooked with a little olive oil until just wilted, and pour the sauce around.

Beurre blanc

¼ cup dry white wine
2 teaspoons white wine vinegar
2 small shallots, finely chopped
2 tablespoons heavy cream
⅔ cup cold unsalted butter, cubed
salt and pepper

Put the wine, vinegar, and shallots in a thick-bottomed saucepan, bring to a boil, and reduce by half. Then add the cream and boil for 1 minute. Lower the heat and gradually whisk in the cubes of cold butter. Pass through a fine sieve and season with salt and pepper.

Roast rib of veal glazed with herb crust, tomato and olive sauce

Serves 6

6 ribs of veal, trimmed
(½lb each with the bone)
salt and pepper
4 tablespoons olive oil

Heat the oven to 400°F. Season the veal and place in a heated roasting pan with the oil. Seal well on both sides, then place in the oven for 12 minutes—turn after 6 minutes—for pink-cooked meat. Cover with tin foil and let rest in a warm place for 10–15 minutes before serving.

Cut ¼in thick slices of the herb crust and roll it out between two sheets of plastic wrap, to the size of the chops—you may have to cut and reshape the crust as the chops are rarely perfect circles. Place the chops under a hot broiler until the crust bubbles and starts to turn crisp and brown. Serve immediately on a pool of sauce antiboise (page 132). Broiled confit potatoes are an excellent accompaniment, together with little garlic flans.

Herb and pepper crust

1oz each of basil, chives, parsley, rosemary, tarragon and thyme
1½ tablespoons black and white peppercorns
1 cup butter, softened
¼lb beef bone marrow (or butter)
3 cups dry white bread crumbs
1¼ cups Gruyère cheese, grated
¾ cup Cheddar cheese, grated

Wash and dry the herbs, then roughly chop. Crush the peppercorns. Put the herbs, peppercorns, softened butter, and all the remaining ingredients into a blender and blend until smooth. Form the mixture into a large sausage shape, wrap in plastic wrap, and tie both ends. Freeze until ready to use.

Wine suggestion:
Domaine Richeaume Cuvée Tradition
1998, Henning Hoesch

Sauce antiboise

9 ripe plum tomatoes

16 each of black, green
and purple olives

3 tablespoons tomato fondue
(page 64)

1 shallot, finely chopped

1 garlic clove, chopped

½ cup strong Provençal extra
virgin olive oil

juice of ½ lemon

12 basil leaves

Blanch the tomatoes in boiling water for 15 seconds, then peel, cut in half, and scoop out the seeds. Cut the flesh into ⅛in dice. Remove the olive pits by pressing the olives between thumb and forefinger.

Warm the tomato fondue in a saucepan over low heat, then add the diced tomatoes, chopped shallot, garlic, and olive oil. Do not boil, otherwise the scent of the olive oil will be lost. Check for seasoning and, just before serving, add the lemon juice, shredded basil leaves, and olives.

Garlic flan

3 heads of garlic

2 eggs and 1 egg yolk

scant ½ cup milk

scant ½ cup heavy cream

salt and white pepper

Peel the garlic, cut each clove in half, and remove any green shoots. Place in a saucepan, cover with cold salted water, and bring to a boil; drain, and repeat three times. Drain the garlic and push it through a fine sieve into a bowl. Whisk in the eggs, milk, and cream, season and let rest for 15 minutes. Pour into well buttered dariole molds (1½in deep x 1in diameter) and cook in a water bath at 250°F for 35 minutes.

Grilled confit potatoes

12 Charlotte or Belle de Fontenay
potatoes

1 tablespoon olive oil

1 lb 6oz duck or goose fat

Peel the potatoes and, with a small knife, shape into small ovals with flat surfaces. Heat a ribbed broiler and very lightly oil the potatoes; place on the broiler and cook until well scorched, then lift and turn through 90 degrees; place back on the broiler. Turn the potatoes over and repeat, so there is a latticed broiler mark on both sides. Place them in the melted goose fat and simmer for 30 minutes or until tender. Leave in the fat until needed. Drain and sprinkle with coarse sea salt.

Chicken with lentils and thyme

Serves 4

1 cup Puy lentils

1 carrot

1 onion, peeled and cut in half

1 celery stalk

1 garlic clove

½lb smoked bacon

1 bouquet garni

3⅔ cups chicken stock (page 264)

olive oil

12 baby turnips

12 baby new season onions (grelot onions—the type that look like bulbous scallions)

1 free-range or organic chicken

½ cup butter

2 cups chicken jus (page 268)

12 white mushrooms

3 tablespoons fresh thyme leaves

salt and pepper

This is very simple to make and delicious at any time of year. In summer it is excellent cold, served with a leafy salad dressed with walnut oil.

Soak the lentils in cold water for 1 hour. Drain and put in a wide pan with the carrot, onion, celery, garlic, half the bacon, the bouquet garni, and stock. Bring to a boil and then simmer for approximately 30 minutes or until tender (you may need to top up with a little water if necessary). Drain and set aside.

While the lentils are simmering, cut the remaining bacon into large lardons, place in cold water, and bring to a boil for 1 minute. Drain and refresh in cold water, then pat dry. Fry in a hot non-stick pan, adding a little oil to prevent sticking, until the lardons begin to crisp.

Peel the turnips and blanch in boiling water for 3–4 minutes. Blanch the grelot onions for 2–3 minutes.

Joint the chicken and pan fry with a little butter until three-quarters cooked.

Bring the chicken jus to a boil in an enameled cast-iron pot. Add the lentils, turnips, baby onions, and mushrooms, and finally the chicken. Simmer for 10 minutes, or until the chicken is cooked. Add the remaining butter, cut into small pieces, and the thyme. Check for seasoning and serve hot.

Spicy raw beef with quail's eggs

Serves 4

1 ¾lb sirloin steak (14oz for
appetizer)
12 cornichons (small French
pickles), chopped
6 shallots, finely chopped
1 tablespoon super-fine capers
1 tablespoon ketchup
1 tablespoon Dijon mustard
2 tablespoons mayonnaise
2 tablespoons chopped parsley
dash of brandy
Worcestershire and Tabasco sauce
salt
4 quail's eggs
3–4oz cooked truffle, thinly sliced

Use sirloin steak, as the grain of the meat is not as stringy as fillet and not as chewy as topside. The beef should be of the best quality, never frozen and matured for only 1 week. All the ingredients can be prepared in advance; even the meat can be chopped a few hours before serving as long as it is kept cold, but the mixing must be done at the last minute.

Remove any sinew and fat from the sirloin, then with a sharp, thin-bladed knife cut into thin slices. Lay these flat on a chopping board and cut into strips, then cut across to make very small dice. You can use an electric mincer, but I find it changes the texture of the meat. Put the chopped steak into a big bowl in the refrigerator.

Just before serving, mix the pickles, shallots, capers, ketchup, mustard, mayonnaise, parsley, and brandy with the chopped meat and season with Worcestershire and Tabasco sauce and salt to taste. Divide the meat into four and shape into patties.

I like to place some thinly sliced truffle and a soft-boiled quail's egg on top and serve with a curly endive salad, French fries or a crispy potato galette (page 192). Drizzle the plate with sour cream thinned down with a little cold water.

Wine suggestion:
Château de Selle (rosé) 1999,
Domaine Ott

Roast rack of pork, charcutière sauce

Serves 8

1 rack of organic pork (8 bones
from the neck end)

salt

4 tablespoons olive oil

¾ cup butter

24 new potatoes such as Charlotte
or Vivaldi

24 garlic cloves

4 sprigs of thyme

2 bay leaves

1 cup dry white wine

1 tablespoon white wine vinegar

4 shallots, chopped

1¼ cups veal stock (page 264)

1 tablespoon cracked black and
white pepper

1 tablespoon Dijon grain mustard

8 plum tomatoes, peeled,
deseeded and diced

4 tablespoons cornichons (small
French gherkins), thinly sliced

Rack of pork, if cooked slightly pink and left to rest in a warm place for at least 45 minutes, is truly delicious. Make sure the pork is of the best quality, score the skin and rub salt into it if you want crackling. Or ask the butcher to remove the skin and cook a separate confit of belly of pork (opposite) to make the best cracklings ever.

Heat the oven to 375°F. Season the rack of pork and cover the tips of the bones with tin foil to protect them from burning. Place in a hot roasting pan with the olive oil and ½ cup of butter, and roast in the oven for 30 minutes. After 5 minutes, put the peeled potatoes, garlic cloves in their skins, thyme, and bay leaves into the roasting pan and season lightly. Make sure the roasting pan is large enough to accommodate all the ingredients without them being squashed.

After 30 minutes, turn down the oven to 300°F and roast for a further 15 minutes, basting often. Remove the pork, cover with tin foil, and let rest in a warm place for 45 minutes. The new potatoes and garlic should by now be golden: If not, turn the oven up to 400°F and put the pan back in the oven for another 5 minutes. Remove the potatoes and garlic and keep warm.

To make the charcutière sauce, discard the fat from the roasting pan, pour in the wine and vinegar and bring to a boil, scraping the pan with a spatula to loosen all the caramelized juices. In another pan, sweat the shallots with ¼ cup of butter, then strain the wine on to the shallots, add the veal stock and cracked pepper, and reduce by two-thirds. Whisk in the remaining butter and mustard, and stir in the diced tomatoes. Finally just before serving, add the cornichons. Take the rack of pork to the table and carve into chops.

Pork belly cracklings

Take a belly of top quality pork: not too fatty but nonetheless with a good depth of fat, such as from the Middle White breed. Remove the bones, score the skin, and cut into $1\frac{1}{2}$in x $3\frac{1}{2}$in chunks. Sprinkle liberally with coarse sea salt and place in the refrigerator for 90 minutes.

Brush off and discard the salt. Melt about $2\frac{1}{4}$lb of duck fat in a large saucepan, adding a small cheesecloth bag filled with a few sprigs of sage, some cracked white pepper, and 2 crushed garlic cloves. Plunge the pork into the fat and simmer gently for 90 minutes or until tender. Let cool in the fat. The confit can be kept in its fat in the refrigerator for months.

To cook, place in a non-stick roasting pan, loosely cover with tin foil and roast in a hot oven (400°F) for 15 minutes, turning twice. The result is crisp, yet melt-in-the-mouth, tender pork.

Stuffed saddle of lamb
with spinach and garlic, saffron jus

Serves 6–8

1 saddle of lamb (with kidneys)
½lb caul fat
salt and pepper
20 garlic cloves, peeled
½ cup butter
olive oil for roasting
½ cup heavy cream
2lb spinach
2 egg yolks
1 large onion, chopped
½ cup sweet white wine
2 pinches of saffron strands
2 cups chicken stock (page 264)

Remove the skin and excess fat from the lamb. Bone the saddle of lamb from the belly, removing the fillets but without making any holes on the upper side; this is a slightly tricky task. Cut the flaps to 4½in on each side, lay the saddle on the stretched caul fat, and season lightly. Chop all the bones.

Heat the oven to 400°F. Blanch the garlic in boiling salted water for 1 minute, then drain. Put the garlic on a sheet of tin foil with a tablespoon of butter and a little oil, season, then fold over and seal the tin foil and place in a hot oven for 20 minutes. Let cool. Boil the cream until reduced by half and let cool. Blanch the spinach in boiling salted water. Refresh under cold running water, squeeze completely dry, and chop roughly. Cut the lamb kidneys into small dice, toss in a hot non-stick pan for 15 seconds, then drain and add to the spinach, together with the cream, egg yolks, and roasted garlic. Turn up the oven to 425°F.

Spoon some of the spinach mixture down the center of the boned lamb saddle, place the fillets on top, and cover with the remaining spinach. Roll the belly flaps over the center, wrap in the caul fat, and tie with string. Roast in the oven for 30 minutes, then remove from the oven and let the meat rest in a warm place for at least 30 minutes.

Meanwhile, drain the fat from the roasting pan and add the bones and onion with a little fresh olive oil. Cook over medium heat, stirring frequently. When browned, deglaze with the wine, and allow to reduce by half. Add the saffron and stock and reduce by two-thirds, skimming off the fat. Strain into a clean saucepan and whisk in a little butter to thicken and shine the sauce. Serve immediately with the lamb.

Poached white peaches in Tokaji wine

Serves 10

8–10 white peaches
(depending on size)
2 cups Tokaji wine
1½ cups caster sugar
4 vanilla beans
biscuit cuillère (page 143)
1 cup whipping cream
¼ cup confectioner's sugar

Tokaji jelly
2 cups Tokaji wine
1¼ cups caster sugar
5 sheets of gelatin

Blanch the peaches in boiling water for 10–15 seconds to loosen the skins, then refresh in ice-cold water. Peel and slice into segments.

Put the wine and sugar in a saucepan. Split the vanilla beans and scrape out the seeds into the pan with the wine and sugar, add the pods, and bring to a boil. Poach the peaches in the wine syrup for 2–3 minutes, until tender but still holding their shape—not all the peaches will fit in one go so do this in several batches. Once cooked, let the peaches drain on a rack over a tray in the refrigerator for at least 3 hours; do not pile them up on top of each other or they will lose shape.

For the Tokaji jelly, warm the wine and sugar until the sugar dissolves, but do not boil. Soften the gelatin in cold water, squeeze dry, then whisk into the warm Tokaji and set aside.

Pass the liquid that has drained from the peaches through a fine sieve to use as the sauce (any left over can be mixed with Champagne for a summer cocktail).

Line individual flan rings (2¼in diameter x 1½in deep) with plastic wrap and put a round of biscuit cuillère at the bottom. Loosely fill the rings with the peaches and spoon over the cold but not set Tokaji jelly, filling the rings to ¼in from the top. Refrigerate for at least 2 hours to set.

Whisk the cream with the confectioner's sugar; fill the rings to the brim with this sweetened cream, then smooth off with a palette knife. To serve, place each flan ring in a deep plate then remove the rings. Pour a little sauce around and decorate with a honey tuile (page 49).

Strawberry and red wine gelatin

Serves 8

3½ cups strawberries

1 bottle of Beaujolais or similar
light red wine

1–1¼ cups caster sugar
(depending on the sweetness of the
strawberries)

1 sprig of basil

5 cracked white peppercorns

8 sheets of gelatin

If necessary, wash the strawberries before hulling; if they are large, cut in half, otherwise leave whole.

Bring the wine to a boil with the sugar, basil, and pepper, then remove from the heat. Soften the gelatin in cold water, squeeze dry, then whisk into the wine syrup; set aside. When nearly cold, pass through a fine sieve and bring back to a simmer; add the strawberries and immediately remove from the heat. Let cool to hand hot.

Pour the gelatin and strawberries into individual molds (2¼in diameter x 1½in deep), filling them to the rim, and leave in the refrigerator for at least 2 hours to set. Before the gelatin is completely set, place a circle of biscuit cuillère, cut to the same size as the mold, on the bottom of the gelatin.

To serve, dip the molds briefly in hot water, then invert, and serve with crème anglaise (page 280).

Biscuit cuillère

2 eggs, separated

3 tablespoons caster sugar

6 tablespoons all-purpose flour

confectioner's sugar

Heat the oven to 425°F. Whisk the egg yolks with two-thirds of the caster sugar to a ribbon consistency. Beat the whites until firm but not stiff, then beat in the remaining caster sugar until stiff. Fold one-third of the whites into the yolks until well mixed, then fold in the remaining whites, but before they are completely mixed add the sifted flour and gently fold until the mixture just becomes perfectly smooth. Using a palette knife, spread on a sheet of non-stick baking paper to a thickness of ¼in, dust with confectioner's sugar, and cook in the hot oven for 8 minutes.

Hot cherries with chocolate brownie and pistachio ice cream

Serves 10

1¼ cups red wine
½ cup sugar
1¾lb cherries, pitted

Bring the wine and sugar to a boil, add the cherries, and boil for 20 seconds, then remove the cherries. Boil the liquid to reduce until syrupy. Return the cherries to the syrup and keep warm.

Chocolate brownies

9½oz extra bitter unsweetened chocolate, chopped
1 cup unsalted butter
2 cups caster sugar
1 teaspoon vanilla extract
½ teaspoon salt
5 eggs
1¾ cups all-purpose flour

Heat the oven to 300°F. In a large bowl set over a saucepan of simmering water, melt the chocolate and butter together and then whisk in the sugar, vanilla, and salt. Beat in the eggs, two at a time. Fold in the sifted flour. Pour into individual buttered rings (2¾in diameter x ¾in deep) and cook for 12 minutes, until set on the outside but slightly undercooked and moist in the middle.

To serve: Decorate the plates with a little melted chocolate in a piping bag. Place a warm brownie in the middle of each plate and arrange the hot cherries with the wine syrup around. Finish with a big scoop of pistachio ice cream (see page 252) and a few chopped pistachio nuts.

Wine suggestion:
Banyuls, Cuvée Léon Parcé,
Domaine de la Rectorie

Vanilla flavored creamed rice with stewed peaches

Serves 8

⅞ cup pudding rice

2–2½ cups milk

2 vanilla beans, split

⅓ cup caster sugar

3 tablespoons heavy cream

7 fl oz condensed milk

3 tablespoons butter

4 ripe peaches

Rinse the rice in cold water and drain. Bring 2 cups of the milk to a boil with the vanilla beans and sugar, add the rice, and simmer for 30 minutes, stirring occasionally; you may need to add a little more milk to keep it moist. Set aside for 5 minutes. Finish the rice by stirring in the cream, condensed milk, and butter.

Plunge the peaches into boiling water for 10 seconds to loosen the skins, then refresh immediately in ice-cold water; this enables you to remove the skins without damaging the flesh or using a peeler. Cut the peaches into six wedges, sprinkle with a little sugar, and stew in a saucepan over moderate heat. The amount of sugar depends on taste and how sweet the peaches are; they should not take more than 10 minutes to cook.

To serve: Reheat the rice if necessary: It may become a little stodgy, but if this happens just add a drop of warm milk to thin it down. Serve the rice in small deep plates with a big spoonful of the peach compote. Decorate with a sesame and poppy tuile (page 49) shaped as a curved triangle.

Wine suggestion:
Condrieu 'Les Eguets' Récoltes Tardives
1996, Yves Cuilleron

Ice creams

Serves 12 (3 scoops each)
1 quart whole milk
4 vanilla beans, split
12 egg yolks
1¼ cups caster sugar
2 teaspoons vanilla extract

Vanilla ice cream

Bring the milk to a boil with the vanilla beans. Remove from the heat, cover, and let infuse for 10 minutes.

Beat the egg yolks with the sugar until thick and creamy. Bring the milk back to a boil and pour on to the yolk mixture, whisking continuously. Pour the mixture back into the saucepan and cook over low heat, stirring continuously with a rubber spatula, until the custard thickens slightly. Stir in the vanilla extract and pass through a fine sieve. Chill, then churn in an ice-cream machine until frozen.

Lemon verbena ice cream

Follow the recipe for vanilla ice cream, omitting the vanilla beans and extract. While the custard is still hot, add ¼lb of dried lemon verbena leaves, cover, and let cool. Pass through a fine sieve, then churn in an ice-cream machine.

Lavender ice cream

Nothing can beat the taste of wild lavender picked in the *garrigues* of Provence. Lacking this, make sure to use untreated lavender flowers. Wash the flowers well in cold water and let dry before using.

Follow the recipe for vanilla ice cream, omitting the vanilla beans and extract. While the custard is still hot, add 2oz (or more for a stronger flavor) of lavender flowers. Cover and let steep until the mixture is cold. Pass through a fine sieve, pressing well to extract all the flavor from the flowers—or you can leave the flowers in the mix—then churn in an ice-cream machine.

Honey ice cream

Serves 8 (3 scoops each)

2 cups milk

4 egg yolks

1 ¼ cups flower-scented clear honey

1 ¼ cups heavy cream

Bring the milk to a boil in a saucepan. Meanwhile, whisk the yolks with the honey until thick and creamy, then slowly whisk in the cream. Pour the boiling milk on to the yolk mixture and whisk vigorously. Strain the mixture and let cool. Chill, then churn in an ice-cream machine.

Bitter chocolate ice cream

Serves 8

2 cups whole milk

3 tablespoons unsweetened cocoa powder

½ cup light brown sugar

2 vanilla beans, split

½ lb bitter chocolate (70% cocoa solids), chopped

4 tablespoons crème fraîche

Bring the milk, cocoa powder, sugar, and vanilla beans to a boil, stirring continuously with a whisk. Remove the vanilla beans, scrape out any seeds, and add to the milk. Add the chopped chocolate and stir until completely melted. Let cool slightly. When lukewarm add the crème fraîche, then churn in an ice-cream machine.

Milk chocolate and malt ice cream

Serves 12

2 ¾ cups whole milk

1 cup heavy cream

4 egg yolks

3 tablespoons caster sugar

11 oz milk chocolate (32–36% cocoa solids), melted

⅔ cup liquid malt extract (available from health food shops)

Bring the milk and cream to a boil in a saucepan. Beat the egg yolks with the sugar until creamy, and then slowly pour the hot milk on to the yolks, whisking continuously. Pour the mixture back into the saucepan and cook over low heat, stirring continuously with a wooden spatula, until the mixture thickens slightly. Remove from the heat and stir in the melted chocolate and malt extract until evenly mixed. Chill, then churn in an ice-cream machine.

Caramel ice cream

Serves 6

1¾ cups whole milk

5 egg yolks

3 tablespoons caster sugar

For the caramel

½ cup sugar

½ cup light cream

Bring the milk to a boil in a saucepan. Whisk the yolks and sugar together until thick and creamy. Pour the boiling milk on to the egg mixture, whisking continuously, then return to the saucepan and cook over low heat, stirring continuously with a wooden spatula, until the mixture thickens enough to coat the spatula. Remove from the heat and pass through a fine sieve.

In a separate, thick-bottomed saucepan, cook the sugar over high heat until it caramelizes. When the caramel is dark brown, gently pour in the cream, whisking continuously; beware, as the cream may bubble over if poured too quickly. Pass through a sieve into the first mixture, leave until cold, then churn in an ice-cream machine until frozen.

Banana and rum ice cream

Serves 12

2¼lb very ripe bananas (peeled weight)

3 cups caster sugar

¾ cup good-quality dark rum

juice of 1 lemon

1 quart light cream

If the bananas are not fully ripe, leave them in a warm place or even a very low oven for 3 hours.

Peel the bananas and blend in a food processor or blender with the sugar, rum and lemon juice. Slowly add the cream, blending until smooth. Pour into an ice-cream machine and churn until frozen.

Fresh mint ice cream with chocolate chips

Serves 12 (3 scoops each)
1 quart milk
12 egg yolks
1 cup caster sugar
½lb fresh mint leaves
1–2 tablespoons green mint liqueur
14oz unsweetened bitter chocolate

Bring the milk to a boil. Beat the egg yolks with the sugar until thick and creamy. Pour the hot milk on to the yolk mixture, whisking continuously. Pour the mixture back into the saucepan and cook over low heat, stirring continuously with a rubber spatula, until the mixture thickens slightly. Pour the hot custard on to the mint leaves and let infuse until cold. Pass through a fine sieve, pressing well to extract all the flavor of the mint. Add the mint liqueur, then pour into an ice-cream machine and churn until frozen.

To make the chocolate chips, melt the chocolate and transfer to a piping bag with a very small nozzle. Pipe drops of chocolate on to a sheet of wax paper and set in the refrigerator. Fold into the ice cream.

Condensed milk ice cream

Serves 12
3 quarts whole milk
1¼ cups caster sugar
1½ cups condensed milk

Boil the milk and sugar together, stirring occasionally, until reduced by half; in other words there is 1½ quarts left. Stir in the condensed milk and let cool. Churn in an ice-cream machine until frozen.

Raspberry ice cream

Serves 12
5¼ cups unsweetened raspberry purée
2 cups caster sugar
finely grated zest and juice of ½ lemon and ½ orange
⅓ cup Grand Marnier
1 cup heavy cream

Put all the ingredients into a large bowl and mix thoroughly with a whisk. Pour into an ice-cream machine and churn until frozen.

Iced red berry soufflé

Serves 10

*8 cups mixed berries
(e.g., strawberries, raspberries,
blueberries, blackcurrants),
plus extra to decorate
2 cups caster sugar
juice of 1 lemon
4 egg whites
2 cups water
⅓ cup whipping cream*

Hull and, if necessary, wash the fruit. Blend with ⅔ cup of the sugar, then pass through a fine sieve and add lemon juice to heighten the taste if required. Prepare 10 individual soufflé dishes (3½in diameter x 2¼in deep) by tying a piece of wax paper around the edge to form a collar that stands 2in above the rim.

Put the egg whites into the bowl of an electric mixer. In a perfectly clean saucepan, dissolve the remaining 1¼ cups of sugar in the water over low heat. When the sugar has completely dissolved, bring to a boil, skim off the foam, and cook to 250°F on a sugar thermometer. Beat the egg whites until foamy, then, with the whisk still running, pour the hot sugar directly on to the egg whites, avoiding the beaters. Continue beating until the meringue is cool.

Whip the cream until soft peaks form and fold into the fruit pulp. Delicately fold in the meringue, then spoon into the prepared soufflé dishes. Freeze for 12 hours.

Decorate with fresh berries and, if you like, serve with a sauce made by puréeing 7 cups berries with ½cup caster sugar, sharpening the taste with a little lemon juice.

Feuillantines with berries and cream cheese sorbet

Serves 8

1 cup caster sugar
1 lb puff pastry (page 278—
trimmings can be used)
5 cups berries (e.g., blueberries,
wild strawberries, loganberries)
1 cup Chantilly cream (page 280)

Sprinkle a work surface liberally with caster sugar and roll out the pastry to a ⅛in thick rectangle. Roll up the pastry as tightly as possible into a sausage shape, wrap in plastic wrap, and refrigerate for 1 hour.

Heat the oven to 400°F. Cut ¼in thick slices off the roll of pastry and, rolling lightly and briskly, roll out again on a well-sugared surface, to make very thin, roughly oblong shapes. Place on a non-stick baking sheet and cook until golden, caramelized, and crisp. Transfer to a wire rack to cool.

Cream cheese sorbet

1¼ cups caster sugar
¼ cup glucose syrup
2 cups water
3 tablespoons lemon juice
10oz fromage blanc
1 tablespoon heavy cream

Put the sugar, glucose and water in a saucepan over low heat and stir gently to dissolve the sugar and glucose. Set aside and let cool.

Stir in the lemon juice, fromage blanc, and cream, and churn in an ice-cream machine until frozen.

Mango coulis

1 ripe mango
caster sugar
lemon juice

Peel the mango and scrape all the flesh into a blender. Add caster sugar to taste—the amount depends on the sweetness of the mango—and purée until smooth. Pass through a fine sieve into a bowl, and add lemon juice to taste.

To assemble: Serve three feuillantines per person, layering them with mixed berries and Chantilly cream. Serve with a scoop of cream cheese sorbet, drizzled with a spoonful of mango coulis.

Wine suggestion:
Quarts de Chaume Cuvée des Forges
1997, Branchereau

Green tomato tart with caramel ice cream

Serves 6

14–18 green tomatoes,
depending on size
2 tablespoons caster sugar
1 lb puff pastry (page 278)
2 tablespoons melted butter
2 tablespoons light brown sugar

Slice the green tomatoes fairly thickly and sprinkle with the caster sugar. Leave on a wire rack to drain; the sugar will draw out excess moisture.

Divide the puff pastry into six pieces and roll out each piece into a very thin round, about 4½in in diameter. Use a cutter or saucer to cut out perfect circles, then crimp the edges with your thumb and forefinger. Place the pastry circles on a non-stick baking sheet and refrigerate for 30 minutes.

Heat the oven to 425°F. Place ½ tablespoon of crème d'amande on each of the six pastry circles and spread out with the back of a spoon. Arrange the tomato slices in a spiral on each tart, brush with melted butter, and sprinkle with brown sugar. Place in the oven for 12 minutes. Serve immediately, with caramel ice cream (page 152).

Crème d'amande

3 tablespoons unsalted butter,
softened
⅓ cup confectioner's sugar
¼ cup ground almonds
1 tablespoon all-purpose flour,
sifted
1 egg, beaten

Beat the butter until pale and creamy. Sift the confectioner's sugar and almonds together on to a piece of wax paper. Beat the almond mixture, flour, and egg into the butter a little at a time, until the mixture is light and smooth.

Iced nougat with three melons and blueberry sauce

Serves 8

6 egg whites
1 ¼ cups caster sugar
1 ½ cups whipping cream
2 teaspoons vanilla extract
Charentais, Ogen, and watermelon

Break the caramelized hazelnuts into large crumbs with a rolling pin; set aside.

Place the bowl of an electric mixer over a saucepan of simmering water, add the egg whites and sugar, and whisk gently until the mixture is warm, then put the bowl under the mixer and whisk at full speed, until cold. The mixture should be smooth yet firm. Fold in the whipped cream, vanilla extract, and crushed caramelized nuts. Pour into ramekins (2¼in diameter x 2in deep) lined with plastic wrap—or a plastic wrap-lined loaf pan. Freeze for 24 hours.

To assemble: Scoop the melons into little balls using a Parisienne scoop or melon baller. Turn out the iced nougat and decorate with a sesame and poppy tuile (page 49).

Caramelized hazelnuts

⅓ cup caster sugar
½ cup hazelnuts

Put the sugar in a thick-bottomed saucepan over moderate heat to melt, stirring with a wooden spoon until it becomes a golden caramel. Add the nuts and continue to cook until well coated and the caramel bubbles again. Pour on to an oiled baking sheet to set. Store in an airtight container.

Blueberry sauce

3 ½ cups blueberries
½ cup caster sugar
juice of 1 lemon

Blend the fruit and sugar together until smooth, then press through a fine sieve into a bowl and add lemon juice to taste. All soft fruit and berries can be made into sauces in this simple manner; the natural sweetness of the fruit will determine how much or little sugar you add.

Wine suggestion:
Pacherenc du Vic-Bilh 'Brumaire' 1995
Alain Brumont

Apples Blackberries C

Grouse Jerusal

Oysters Part

Swiss cha

Fall

bbage Chestnuts Corn Figs
n artichokes Leeks Mussels
dge Pears Plums Pumpkin
Walnuts Wild mushrooms

Cep pizza with basil

Serves 8;

or 4 as a main course

2 large onions

olive oil

3lb fresh ceps

(porcini mushrooms)

3 garlic cloves, chopped

salt and pepper

1 bunch of basil

2¼ cups Emmental cheese, grated

This is a recipe that I used to make when I was an apprentice. The dough is similar to brioche, rich and supple, and these pizzas are great as an appetizer or main course.

Cut the onions in half and slice thinly, then sweat in a wide, thick-bottomed saucepan with a little olive oil until tender, 12–15 minutes. Remove the ceps' stalks and chop roughly. Add the stalks and chopped garlic to the onions and continue to cook over medium heat, stirring frequently. Season with salt and pepper. When all the moisture has evaporated and the onions are a golden brown color, remove from the heat and add the basil leaves. Let cool.

Heat the oven to 425°F. Divide the dough into eight balls and roll out to approximately ¼in thick. Place the pizza bases on non-stick baking sheets.

Spoon the cooled onion mixture on to the pizzas, leaving at least ¾in clear at the edge. Slice the ceps and place them on the onion mixture, sprinkle with cheese, drizzle a little olive oil on top, and cook for 16–18 minutes. Serve warm.

Pizza dough

1 cake compressed yeast

1½ cups tepid water

½ cup milk

4½ cups bread flour

1½ tablespoons salt

3 tablespoons sugar

2 eggs

⅔ cup butter, melted

Put the yeast into the bowl of an electric mixer with the dough hook attachment. Pour in the tepid water and milk followed by the flour, salt, sugar, and eggs. Mix at low speed for 5 minutes, then pour in the melted butter, increase the speed to medium, and mix for a further 5 minutes. The dough should be elastic, shiny, and smooth. Cover the dough and refrigerate for at least 3 hours.

Creamed artichoke and cep soup

Serves 10

6 large globe artichokes
2 tablespoons dried ceps
(porcini mushrooms)
2 quarts chicken stock (page 264)
1 leek
1 celery stalk
1 large onion
1 cup button mushrooms
1 tablespoon butter
salt and white pepper
½ cup crème fraîche
¼ cup whipping cream

Using a sharp paring knife, trim the artichokes and place the leaves in a deep saucepan. Add the dried ceps, the stock, and 1 quart of water. Bring to a boil and simmer for 1 hour.

Meanwhile, remove the choke from the artichoke hearts and discard. Chop the artichoke hearts, leek, celery, onion, and mushrooms. Sweat the vegetables with the butter until tender, stirring with a wooden spoon.

Pass the artichoke leaf stock through a sieve and add to the vegetables, then simmer for 30 minutes. Blend the vegetables with the stock and pass the soup through a fine sieve. Taste and adjust the seasoning.

To serve: Bring the soup back to a boil, then add all the cream, and froth the soup with a hand blender. Place little piles of garlic ceps in the center of each soup plate and pour the frothy soup around. Serve immediately.

Garlic ceps

2½ cups fresh ceps
2 tablespoons olive oil
1 shallot, finely chopped
1 garlic clove, finely chopped
1 sprig of flat-leaf parsley, finely
chopped

Brush the ceps clean or wipe with a damp cloth and cut into ½in dice. Fry in a little olive oil until golden brown, then add the shallot, garlic, and parsley. Season with salt and pepper and remove from the heat; do not overcook otherwise the garlic and parsley will burn.

Mushroom and basil soup, langoustines with lobster mousse

Serves 6

4¼ cups button mushrooms

⅓ cup butter

15 basil leaves

1 quart chicken stock (page 264)

½lb potatoes, thinly sliced

salt and pepper

18 cooked langoustines

¾lb lobster mousse

1 cup heavy cream

2 teaspoons crème fraîche

Wash the mushrooms and slice thinly, then sweat in the butter with the shredded basil. Remove some of the mushrooms—about 1 tablespoon per person—and set aside as a garnish.

Pour on the chicken stock, add the potatoes, salt and pepper, and boil for 12 minutes. Purée in a blender, then strain through a fine sieve.

Pull off the langoustine heads and scrape out the contents, then, using a teaspoon, fill the head cavities with lobster mousse. Peel the tails. Steam the filled heads and tails for about 8 minutes.

To serve: Bring the soup to a boil, then add all the cream and froth the soup with a hand blender. Pour into soup plates and arrange the mushrooms in the center, with the langoustine tails and stuffed heads around the mushrooms.

Lobster mousse

1 live lobster, preferably Scottish (about 2lb)

1 egg white

1½ cups heavy cream

salt and white pepper

Kill the lobster by inserting the point of a heavy knife between the eyes. Remove the claws and crack open using the back of the knife or a mallet; scoop out all the meat. Using a pair of heavy-duty scissors, cut the tail open from the underside and scrape out all the flesh. The pieces of shell can be reserved to make a sauce for another recipe.

Blend the lobster meat with the egg white until smooth and then press through a fine sieve into a bowl set over ice. Using a spatula, work the cream into the lobster purée a little at a time. The mixture should be smooth and slightly runny. Season lightly with salt and pepper.

Pan-fried foie gras with spiced breadcrumbs

Serves 8

1 pain d'epices
1 lb 9oz duck foie gras
2 tablespoons plain flour
salt and pepper
1 egg, beaten
⅓ cup unsalted butter

Duck glaze

1 ½ tablespoons caster sugar
1 ½ tablespoons sherry vinegar
1 ½ cups duck jus (page 268)
⅓ cup unsalted butter

Wine suggestion:
Noble Reserve 1981, Hopler (Austria)

¾ cup aromatic clear honey
½ cup milk
3 tablespoons caster sugar
3 eggs
1 cup dark rye flour
1 cup plain white flour
2 ½ teapoons baking powder
2 teaspoons mixed spice
2 teaspoons ground ginger
finely grated rind of ½ orange and
½ lemon
2 teaspoons vanilla extract

Thinly slice the pain d'épices, removing the crusts if dark. Place on a rack and let dry in a warm, well-aired place or in a very low oven. When completely dry, make bread crumbs in a blender or by crushing with a rolling pin. Pass the bread crumbs through a coarse sieve.

Heat the oven to 350°F. Cut the foie gras into ¾in thick slices weighing about 2½oz each. Roll them in seasoned flour, then dip in beaten egg and finally in the bread crumbs. Press the crumbs well into the foie gras, making sure it is completely coated.

For the duck glaze, heat the sugar and vinegar over low heat until light brown. Add the duck jus and reduce until syrupy, then whisk in the butter, cut into small pieces.

Fry the foie gras in a little butter over medium heat until the crumbs have started to crisp, gently turn over, then place in the oven for 4 minutes, basting after 2 minutes. Drain on paper towels. Serve hot, with salad leaves and duck glaze.

Pain d'épices

This spicy gingerbread is delicious served warm for breakfast or afternoon tea with a little salted butter from Brittany.

Butter a large loaf pan (9in x 4½in) and line with buttered wax paper. Heat the oven to 325°F.

Heat the honey with the milk until melted; keep warm. In a large bowl, whisk the sugar and eggs together until very light and smooth. Sift all the dry ingredients together. Stir the warm milk and the vanilla extract into the egg mixture, then fold in the dry ingredients. Bake for 30 minutes, then lower the heat to 300°F and continue to bake for 1 hour. Let cool in the pan for 30 minutes, then invert.

Skate ravioli with celery and capers

Serves 6

2 small skate wings
(1¾–2¼lb each)
1 celery heart (the central
stalk with leaves)
salt and pepper
2 shallots, finely chopped
1 cup butter
¾ cup dry white wine
3 tablespoons heavy cream
1 small bunch of parsley,
coarsely chopped
2 tablespoons super-fine capers
2 lemons, all peel and pith cut off,
then segmented

If possible use blonde ray; I find it the best, and it is less likely to smell and taste of ammonia, which is sometimes the case with skate.

Fillet the skate and remove the skin. Slice the skate into very fine slivers, add the very thinly sliced celery heart, keeping a few leaves for decoration, and season with salt and pepper. Divide the mixture into six balls and press together firmly.

Cut the ravioli dough into 12 circles (3½in diameter) and fill with the skate mixture to make six large ravioli. Cook for 2 minutes in salted boiling water, flip them over, and cook for a further 2 minutes.

Meanwhile, sweat the shallots in 2 tablespoons of the butter until well softened. Add the wine and reduce by two-thirds. Add the cream, bring to a boil, and whisk in the remaining butter, cut into pieces. Season with salt and pepper and stir in the chopped parsley, capers, and lemon segments. Serve the ravioli on warmed plates, pour the sauce around, and decorate with a few celery leaves.

Ravioli dough

2¼ cups bread flour
pinch of salt
3 large egg whites

Sift the flour and salt on to a work surface, add the egg whites, and knead until smooth and elastic, adding a little water if needed: The paste should be elastic but not sticky. Let rest for 2 hours before use.

Using a pasta machine, roll out as thinly as possible.

Wine suggestion:
*Pouilly-Fuissé 'Vieilles Vignes' 1998,
Domaine Cordier*

Mille-feuille of mussels and baby spinach

Serves 4

½lb puff pastry (page 278)
12oz baby spinach leaves
5 quarts fresh mussels
2 cups dry white wine
1 onion, finely chopped
3 tablespoons butter
2 teaspoons Madras curry powder
1 small bouquet garni
½ cup heavy cream
salt and pepper

Look for 'bouchot' (pole-grown) mussels or rope-grown mussels; these have a good flavor and are unlikely to be sandy.

On a lightly floured work surface, roll out the puff pastry to a thickness of ⅛in. Cut in half, cover, and let rest in the refrigerator for 20 minutes.

Heat the oven to 350°F. Put the pastry on a baking sheet and prick with a fork, then put another baking sheet on top, and cook for 15 minutes. Remove the top sheet and cook for a further 5 minutes, until brown and crisp. Let cool, then cut into 12 rectangles (2½in x 1½in).

Wash the spinach and dry in a salad spinner; handle it carefully as it is very delicate.

Wash the mussels in plenty of cold water. Put them in a hot saucepan with the wine, cover, and cook over high heat, shaking the pan from time to time. When all the mussels have opened (6–8 minutes), drain them in a colander set over a bowl to collect the cooking liquid. Shell the mussels.

Sweat the onion with the butter, curry powder, and bouquet garni until tender. Add the mussel cooking liquid and bring to a boil; reduce by a third, then add the cream and continue to reduce to a light sauce consistency. Reheat the mussels in this sauce without boiling, remove the bouquet garni, and check the seasoning.

In a wide frying pan, lightly cook the spinach with a drop of olive oil until just wilted. Season with salt and pepper.

To assemble: Build the "mille-feuille" on four warmed plates, with the spinach, mussels, and sauce in between the three layers of puff pastry.

Wine suggestion:
Alsace Riesling 'Cuvée des Comtes d'Eguisheim' 1998, Léon Beyer

171

Seared peppered tuna with caviar vinaigrette

Serves 4

9oz tuna loin

coarsely ground black and white pepper

a little olive oil

12 dried tomato halves (page 273)

2½oz oscietre caviar

¼lb baby spinach leaves

olive oil vinaigrette

Cut the tuna into long cylindrical fillets, about 1in in diameter. Roll them in the "mignonette" of mixed pepper, pressing lightly, then season with salt and sear in a hot, thick-bottomed frying pan with a little olive oil until cooked very rare.

To serve: Cut the seared tuna into ½in thick slices and arrange on the plates with the dried tomatoes, brushed with olive oil. Pour a little caviar vinaigrette around the tuna and place a teaspoon of caviar on each slice of tuna. Lightly toss the spinach in a good olive oil vinaigrette. Serve the spinach between two potato galettes in the center of each plate.

Potato galettes

1 Desirée or Maris Piper potato

olive oil

Peel and wash the potatoes, then grate or shred finely. Divide into eight and shape by pressing into a 1½in diameter cutter. Cook in a small, thick-bottomed frying pan with a little olive oil until crisp on both sides.

Caviar vinaigrette

1 cup grapeseed oil

1 egg yolk

1–2 teaspoons Dijon mustard

1–2 teaspoons sherry vinegar

3 tablespoons water

2½oz pressed caviar

salt and pepper

Whisk together the oil, egg yolk, mustard, vinegar, and water until smooth. Stir in the caviar and season to taste.

Any leftover vinaigrette can be kept, sealed, in the refrigerator for up to 2 weeks. It can be served with smoked salmon, lobster, or any cold fish salad.

Wine suggestion:
Châteauneuf-du-Pape (blanc)
'Clos des Papes' 1995, Paul Avril

Cockle risotto with flat parsley

Serves 4

2¼lb fresh cockles in their shells

1¼ cups dry white wine

1 cup chicken stock (page 264)

2 shallots, finely chopped

2 tablespoons unsalted butter

⅞ cup arborio rice

⅓ cup Parmesan cheese, grated

1 tablespoon mascarpone

salt and pepper

1oz flat-leaf parsley, coarsely chopped

Wash the cockles in several changes of cold water, scrubbing the shells if necessary. Put them in a hot saucepan with 1 cup of the wine, cover the pan, and cook over high heat, shaking the pan from time to time. When all the shells have opened (6–8 minutes), drain into a colander set over a bowl to collect the cooking liquid. Remove the cockles from their shells and set aside. Bring the chicken stock to a boil and set aside.

In a thick-bottomed saucepan, sweat the shallots with the butter until translucent but not browned. Add the rice and cook for a few seconds, stirring until the rice is translucent.

Pour in the remaining wine and turn up the heat until the wine has evaporated, stirring constantly. Then add a ladleful of the hot cockle cooking liquid and turn down the heat to a simmer. Continue adding the cockle liquid, then the hot chicken stock, a little at a time, stirring occasionally, until all the stock is absorbed and the rice is tender.

Remove from the heat and stir in the cockles, Parmesan, and mascarpone. Season to taste, add the parsley, and serve immediately, on warmed plates.

Wine suggestion:
Pinot Grigio 1998, Jermann (Italy)

Scallops in a cream rosemary sauce, wild rice with squid

Serves 6

18 large scallops in the shell
3 shallots, sliced
1 cup dry white wine
2 sprigs of rosemary
1¼ cups heavy cream
2 tablespoons crème fraîche
salt and pepper
lemon juice

Wine suggestion:
*Condrieu 'Les Chaillets' Vieilles Vignes
1996, Yves Cuilleron*

Open the scallops, separate the corals, and trim off the sinews and membranes. Discard the black parts, then soak the trimmings in cold water for 1 hour. Rinse well to remove any traces of sand, then drain. Rinse the scallops and pat dry.

Put the shallots in a saucepan with the wine, rosemary, and scallop trimmings, boil for 2 minutes, then add water to cover and simmer for 20 minutes. Strain through a fine sieve into a clean pan, pressing well to extract all the flavors. Reduce by half, then add both creams, season with salt and pepper, and reduce for 4 minutes to a rich sauce consistency.

Slice the scallops in half and drop them into the sauce; simmer gently for 1 minute, but do not boil. Using a slotted spoon, remove the scallops and arrange on warmed plates.

Bring the sauce back to a boil, whisk in a few drops of lemon juice, and then pour over the scallops. Garnish with blanched baby new season onions, turned carrots, and lightly sautéed button mushrooms.

Wild rice with squid

½ cup wild rice
3 baby squid
1 small onion, finely chopped
1 red bell pepper, peeled and diced
1 tablespoon butter
*2½ cups chicken stock
(page 264), or mussel or lobster
stock (page 267)*
salt

Heat the oven to 325°F. Rinse the rice in cold water and drain well. Chop the squid tentacles and cut the body into rings. Sweat the onion and pepper with the butter in an ovenproof pan for 5 minutes. Add the rice and cook, stirring, for 2 minutes. Pour in 1¾ cups of the stock and bring to a boil. Cover with buttered wax paper and place in the oven for about 40 minutes; stir every 15 minutes, adding a little more stock if dry. The rice should be tender and just starting to crack open. Stir in a pat of butter and salt to taste. If you like, pack into dariole molds, then invert.

Sole poached with saffron and cilantro

Serves 4

2 Dover soles (2¼lb each)
salt and pepper
1 bunch of fresh cilantro,
leaves finely chopped
2 tablespoons butter
2 shallots, chopped
1 cup dry white wine
generous pinch of saffron strands
⅔ cup heavy cream

Heat the oven to 350°F.

Skin and fillet the soles, lightly score the skin side with a sharp knife, then gently flatten with a cleaver, just enough to break the fibers and give an even thickness. Season the skin side and sprinkle with the chopped cilantro leaves. Roll up the fillets and secure each one with a wooden toothpick.

Butter an ovenproof dish, add the chopped shallots, wine, and soles, and bring to a gentle simmer. Cover with wax paper and place in the oven. After 3–4 minutes, turn the roulades and cook for a further 4 minutes.

Remove from the oven and drain the cooking liquid into a hot saucepan. Add the saffron and reduce by two-thirds. Add the cream and reduce to a fairly rich sauce consistency.

Remove the toothpicks and cut each fillet in half. Serve on a bed of peeled red bell peppers, cut into strips, and pan-fried in olive oil.

Mick Jagger had shot to world stardom with the Rolling Stones' 'Satisfaction' in 1965. He and singer Marianne Faithfull came to the restaurant in Chelsea soon after we opened in 1967

178

Red mullet with red wine sauce thickened with its liver

Serves 6

6 red mullet (½lb each)

olive oil

salt and pepper

9fl oz red wine sauce (page 269)

3 tablespoons butter, cut

into small pieces

Fillet the red mullet, wash, dry with paper towel, and remove the pin bones using a pair of tweezers. If the red mullet are line-caught or from day boats their delicate bellies will not have been damaged and you will find the livers—these are quite easily recognizable. If there are no livers you can substitute a chicken liver and two anchovy fillets.

Put the fillets, skin side up, on a lightly oiled baking sheet and place under a hot broiler until the skin begins to blister and the fish is cooked.

Bring the red wine sauce to a boil, whisk in the butter and, using a hand blender, incorporate the liver. Pass the sauce through a fine sieve and keep warm; do not re-boil, otherwise the sauce will curdle. Place the fillets on a bed of creamed spinach and serve with saffron potatoes.

Saffron potatoes

Use small new potatoes or "turned" larger ones: Cut into barrel shapes with a paring knife. Cook in salted boiling water with a generous pinch of saffron strands.

Creamed spinach

2¼lb spinach, washed

and picked over

⅓ cup heavy cream

1 garlic clove, finely chopped

salt, nutmeg

Blanch the spinach in boiling salted water for 1 minute; drain and refresh in ice-cold water to retain its color. Drain again and then press dry, using your hands to squeeze out all the moisture. Transfer to a chopping board and chop finely. Bring the cream to a boil, add the garlic, and reduce by half, then add the spinach and heat through. Season to taste with salt and a little freshly grated nutmeg.

Tagine of red mullet and couscous

Serves 8

2 red mullet (1lb 2oz each)

olive oil

salt

1 tablespoon golden raisins

1 cup precooked couscous

1 red chili, finely chopped

2 scallions, sliced

1 garlic clove, finely chopped

a few sprigs of flat-leaf parsley

juice of 1 lime

Heat the oven to 425°F. Fillet the red mullet, wash, dry with paper towel, and remove the pin bones using a pair of tweezers. Cut each fillet into two diamonds and place, skin side up, on a lightly oiled baking sheet; brush a little oil on the fish, and salt sparingly.

Put the golden raisins in a small saucepan, cover with cold water, and bring to a boil. Drain and pat dry. Toast the couscous in hot olive oil for 10 seconds, then pour on enough boiling water for it to absorb. Remove from the heat, add a little more olive oil, and fluff with a fork. Add the chopped chili (with or without the seeds, depending on how hot you like it), scallions, garlic, golden raisins, parsley, lime juice, and salt to taste.

Bake the red mullet in the hot oven for a matter of minutes; the skin should be starting to blister. Spoon the couscous into hot tagine dishes and place a piece of fish on top.

Variation: Put three thin slices of spicy chorizo on top of the red mullet as you bake it.

Poached T-bone of turbot with sauce mousseline

Serves 8–10

1 turbot (about 9–11lb)
court bouillon (page 266)

Using a pair of heavy-duty scissors, remove the fins of the turbot. Then, using a small cleaver or heavy knife, cut off the head and cut in half through the backbone. Then cut across into sections to make the "tronçonettes", or T-bones.

Place the tronçonettes in a wide saucepan with enough court bouillon to cover, quickly bring to a simmer for 2 minutes, then remove from the heat. Leave the fish in the hot liquid for 8–10 minutes, depending on the thickness of the fish; this method of cooking keeps the fish moist and tender.

Gently lift the fish out of the cooking liquid, remove the skin and serve immediately, with the mousseline sauce, spinach, and minted boiled potatoes.

Mousseline sauce

⅓ cup whipping cream
hollandaise sauce (page 270)

Whisk the cream until it forms soft peaks, then fold it into the warm hollandaise sauce.

Mackerel fillet with mussels à la marinière

Serves 4

2 mackerel
1 quart small rope-grown mussels
3 tablespoons butter
12 button mushrooms, sliced
juice of 1 lemon
salt and pepper
1 large mild onion or 4 shallots,
finely chopped
1 celery stalk, finely chopped
1 bay leaf
1 cup dry white wine
3 tablespoons crème fraîche
4 plum tomatoes, peeled,
deseeded, and diced
4 tablespoons coarsely chopped
flat-leaf parsley

Fillet the mackerel, remove the pin bones using a pair of tweezers, then rinse and pat dry. Cut each fillet in half, trimming the edges to neaten. Wash the mussels thoroughly in several changes of cold water, discarding any that are broken or opened.

Melt the butter over high heat and, when foaming, add the mushrooms and lemon juice and season with salt and pepper. As soon as the mushrooms are lightly cooked, remove the pan from the heat.

Put the onion or shallots, celery, bay leaf, mussels, and wine in a very hot saucepan over high heat. Shake the pan and cover with a lid; after 2 minutes stir and shake the pan again. When all the mussels have opened (2–4 minutes), drain them into a colander set over a bowl to collect the cooking liquid. Pick most of the mussels out of their shells, leaving 16 in the shell for decoration.

Put the mussel liquid, including the vegetables, into a smaller saucepan, remove the bay leaf, and add the mushrooms with their juice. Bring to a boil, whisk in the cream, and check the seasoning.

Add the mussels, tomatoes, and parsley. Flood large deep plates with this mussel broth. Pan-fry the mackerel fillets in a non-stick pan with a little olive oil for 20 seconds on each side, then place on the mussels and serve immediately.

Roast mallard, endives, and champagne

Serves 2

1 mallard
salt and pepper
2 tablespoons vegetable oil
2 shallots, thinly sliced
2 heads of chicory, thinly sliced
nutmeg
soft brown sugar
7fl oz champagne
1 cup heavy cream
1 black truffle (optional), sliced

If your duck is still in feather, plucking is not too difficult, as long as you have patience. Grasp little tufts of feathers between your thumb and forefinger and pull firmly but gently, taking care not to rip the skin. Hold the plucked duck over a flame to burn off the down. Remove the wishbone and wing tips and draw out the innards.

Heat the oven to 375°F and place a roasting pan in the oven; add the oil. Season inside the duck cavity with salt and pepper, then place the duck on its back in the hot roasting pan and roast for 10 minutes, then turn it on to its sides for 5 minutes each side; this will give rosy-pink meat. Remove the duck from the pan and turn it breast down so the juices permeate the breast meat; let rest in a warm place.

In the same roasting pan, cook the shallots and chicory with some salt, pepper, freshly ground nutmeg, and the soft brown sugar over high heat, stirring occasionally, until the chicory is a light golden color. Pour in the champagne and reduce by half, then add the cream and reduce by half again, to a light sauce consistency.

Cut off the duck legs and breasts and serve on warmed plates. Tip any duck juices into a boiling champagne sauce, then stir in the sliced truffle, if using. Pour a little sauce over the duck and serve with a gratin of ceps (page 194).

Wine suggestion:
Coteaux du Languedoc 1991, Prieuré de St Jean de Bebian

Corn-fed chicken with saffron milk cap mushrooms and dark rum

Serves 6

4 cups saffron milk cap mushrooms
6 supremes of good-quality
corn-fed chicken, wing tips and
skin on
salt and pepper
vegetable oil
⅓ cup butter
4 shallots, finely sliced
⅓ cup good-quality dark rum
¾ cup crème fraîche

Saffron milk cap mushrooms (*Lactarius deliciosus*) may be found in the fall months in and around pine forests. They should not be eaten raw, as they have a bitter taste that disappears in cooking. They seldom need washing, but should be checked for grit and pine needles, then trimmed with a knife and cut into small pieces.

Season the chicken breasts and cook, skin side down, in a thick-bottomed saucepan with a little oil and half the butter. Cook over medium-high heat until the skin is golden, then turn down the heat and turn the chicken to cook on the other side.

Plunge the mushrooms into salted boiling water for 1 minute, drain in a colander, and pat dry with a cloth.

When the chicken is cooked, remove from the pan and trim the wing tip. Discard the fat from the pan and replace with the remaining butter, then add the mushrooms and shallots, and cook until golden brown. Pour in the rum, boil for 1 minute, then add the crème fraîche and check the seasoning. Boil for 2 minutes, then serve immediately with the chicken breasts and fresh pasta.

Coq à la bière

Serves 4

1 free-range corn-fed chicken
(about 3¼lb)
olive oil and butter
4 shallots, finely chopped
2 cups button mushrooms, sliced
1½ tablespoons brandy
1 bottle (11 fl oz) beer, preferably
dark ale
1 teaspoon brown sugar
7 fl oz heavy cream
salt and pepper

The original version of this dish was made with cockerel (*coq*), but these are not readily available commercially, so this recipe has been adapted to use a free-range (preferably organic) chicken.

Heat the oven to 425°F. Put the chicken on its side in an enamel cast-iron pan with a little olive oil and butter and roast for about 40 minutes; baste the bird several times during cooking, turning it on to its other side and finally on to its back, breast upward. When cooked, transfer the chicken on to a plate, breast down so that the juices permeate the meat while it rests.

Discard the fat from the roasting pan and add a pat of fresh butter, place over low heat, and sweat the shallots until translucent, stirring with a wooden spoon. Add the mushrooms and cook for a further 3 minutes. Pour in the brandy and scrape the bottom of the pan with the spoon to deglaze fully. When almost dry pour in the beer and sugar and reduce by half. Add the cream and reduce again to a light sauce consistency. Whisk in 3 tablespoons of butter cut into small pieces to give the sauce sheen. Season to taste with salt and pepper. Carve the chicken and add to the hot sauce.

Game pies

Serves 12

2¼lb trimmed game meat (wild rabbit, venison, hare, grouse, pheasant)

14oz pork belly

1¾lb pork back fat

9oz lean pork shoulder

salt, pepper, and nutmeg

brandy

3¼lb puff pastry dough (page 278)

12 pieces (1in x ¾in) of loin of venison

5oz cooked foie gras (optional), cut into 12 pieces

1 egg, beaten

This can be made with just one type of game, but if you are using only grouse it might be a little strong, so use slightly less and increase the pork shoulder accordingly. As it is going to be minced, seconds, damaged, or old game can be used.

Make sure all the meat is free of bones and big pieces of sinew, remove the rind from the pork belly and the back fat. Cut the game and all the pork into ¾in dice, season well with salt, pepper, a little nutmeg, and a generous splash of brandy, mix thoroughly, cover with plastic wrap, and refrigerate for at least 36 hours—but no more than 72 hours.

Put the marinated meats through a medium-sized hole on a mincer. Take a third of this mixture and push it through the mincer again, keeping everything as cold as possible, then mix by hand to bring the forcemeat together. Fry a little patty of forcemeat to check for seasoning.

Roll out the pastry to ⅛in thick, and cut out twelve 6in discs. Place a ball of forcemeat on each disc. Push a piece of venison—and foie gras if you are using it—into the forcemeat and top with more forcemeat; this should come to about 1in from the edge of the pastry. Brush the edge of the pastry with beaten egg, then fold over to completely envelope the forcemeat. Pinch the pastry well to seal, then place, seal side down, on a baking sheet lined with non-stick baking paper. Put in the refrigerator to rest for at least 1 hour.

Heat the oven to 350°F. Brush the pastry dough with beaten egg and score with the point of a knife to decorate. Cook for 25 minutes or until hot in the middle; test by inserting a darning needle for 6 seconds. Serve hot or cold, accompanied by sauce poivrade (page 245).

Wine suggestion:
Cuvée Syrah 1995,
Château de Fonsalette

Braised leg of rabbit with olives

Serves 6

4 tablespoons olive oil
6 rabbit legs
salt and pepper
1 onion, finely sliced
2 garlic cloves, chopped
1 bay leaf
1 teaspoon tomato paste
½ cup dry white wine
6 ripe tomatoes, peeled, deseeded,
and chopped
2½ cups chicken stock (page 264)
12 baby new season onions (these
look like bulbous scallions)
6 very thin slices of Parma
or Bayonne ham
30 black and green olives, pitted
1 tablespoon fresh thyme leaves
1 tablespoon butter

Heat a wide thick-bottomed pan, add half the olive oil, and sear the seasoned rabbit legs on all sides over high heat.

Drain off the fat and replace with a tablespoon of fresh oil, add the onion, and turn down the heat. Cook until tender, 5–6 minutes, then add the garlic and cook for a further 2 minutes. Add the bay leaf, tomato paste, and wine, and boil for 1 minute, then add the chopped tomatoes and stock, cover with wax paper, and simmer for 35–45 minutes, until the rabbit is tender. Remove the pan from the heat, leaving the rabbit in the sauce for at least 20 minutes.

Peel the baby onions, leaving at least 1in of the green stalk on. Blanch in boiling water, then cut each one into four, and pan-fry in a little olive oil in a non-stick pan to caramelize.

Remove the rabbit from the casserole dish, cover, and keep warm. Lay the ham on an oiled baking sheet and broil until crisp. While the ham is broiling, press the sauce through a coarse sieve into a clean pan, add the caramelized onions, the olives, thyme, and a couple of pats of butter, and bring back to a boil. Place a slice of ham on each rabbit leg, spoon the sauce around, and serve with gnocchi.

Potato gnocchi

1lb cooked peeled potato (Desirée
or Maris Piper)
3½oz all-purpose flour
1 egg
1 egg yolk
salt and ground white pepper

Boil the potatoes in their skins; let cool, then peel. Push through a sieve and beat in the flour, egg, yolk, salt, and pepper. Put in the refrigerator to rest for 20 minutes.

With lightly floured hands, shape the mixture into balls the size of a big marble and push down with the prongs of a fork.

Cook in boiling salted water; when ready the gnocchi will rise to the surface. Refresh in iced water for 10 seconds and then drain on a cloth. To serve, fry in a non-stick pan with a little olive oil until light golden.

Millefeuille of roast saddle of rabbit with Parmesan

Serves 4

12 baby onions
2 tablespoons butter
2½ cups chicken stock (page 264)
2 cups wild mushrooms
8 baby artichokes
olive oil
1 garlic clove, crushed
1 sprig of thyme
⅔ cup dry white wine
4 saddles of rabbit (domestic, not wild)
salt and pepper
2 tablespoons heavy cream
½ cup Parmesan, grated

Peel the onions and cook in a sauté pan with a little butter and 7fl oz of stock until tender and glazed. Clean and trim the wild mushrooms and cook in a little butter for 2–3 minutes.

Trim the artichokes, leaving a few of the heart leaves. Brown lightly in a little olive oil, then add the garlic, thyme, 3 tablespoons of the wine, and water to cover, and simmer for 12 minutes, until tender.

Heat the oven to 425°F. Cook the seasoned rabbit saddles in a roasting pan with a little olive oil until pink, about 12 minutes. Let rest on a rack for 10 minutes. Remove the loin meat by running a sharp knife down each side of the backbone. Chop the bones and put back into the roasting pan, place over high heat, and deglaze with the rest of the wine. Add the remaining 13fl oz of stock and reduce to a light sauce consistency. Pass through a fine sieve and whisk in a little butter to add gloss.

Boil the cream and whisk in the Parmesan; keep warm.

To assemble: Put a potato galette on each plate. On each one place some mushrooms, two onions, and one loin of rabbit cut into four diamonds. Cover with another potato galette, with the other loin of rabbit similarly cut, one onion and two artichokes, cut in half. Drizzle some Parmesan cream over this and around the millefeuille. Finish with a Parmesan galette (page 59) the same size as the potato galette.

Potato galette

Peel and wash a Desiree or Maris Piper potato, then grate or shred finely. Heat a little olive oil in a small hot frying pan; drop in spoonfuls of the grated potato, press down with a spatula and cook until crispy on both sides.

Wine suggestion:
Cervaro della Sala (Chardonnay)
Antinori (Italy)

Roast rib of beef with cep gratin

Serves 2

*1 rib of beef (about 1¼lb
with the bone)*
olive oil
salt and pepper

I like my beef hung for 21 days on the bone; most butchers
hang meat for 7–14 days, but the extra week ensures
tenderness and gives it the depth of flavor that a rib should
have. Fore rib has a vein of fat running through it that melts as
it cooks to keep the meat beautifully moist and full of flavor.

Heat the oven to 425°F.

Heat a roasting pan over high heat and seal the beef all over
in a little olive oil, then place in the oven and roast for
8 minutes: The meat should be rare. Take out of the oven and
let rest for 10 minutes before serving. Carve at the table and
fight over who has the bone!

Serve with Béarnaise sauce (page 271), a gratin of ceps, and
almond and apricot beignets instead of potato.

Cep gratin

*2 cups fresh ceps
(porcini mushrooms)*
3 tablespoons olive oil
salt and pepper
3 shallots, chopped
1 tablespoon butter
2 slices of Parma ham
1 scallion, chopped
½ garlic clove, chopped
*2 tablespoons chopped
flat-leaf parsley*
*2 tablespoons dry white
bread crumbs*

Heat the oven to 400°F. Trim the ceps, clean with a damp
cloth, then slice thinly and pan-fry in hot olive oil until golden
brown; season and drain in a colander.

Sweat the shallots with the butter, cut the ham into small
dice, and add to the shallots. When the shallots are soft add
the scallion and garlic and cook for a further 2 minutes,
stirring occasionally.

Mix the ceps and parsley with the shallots. Place in a gratin
dish, sprinkle the bread crumbs on top, and bake in the hot
oven for 10 minutes.

Almond and apricot beignets

1 onion, finely chopped

⅓ cup butter, softened

1 ⅓ cups whole organic almonds

4 eggs

4 tablespoons all-purpose flour

8 dried apricots, chopped

2 tablespoons chopped parsley

salt and pepper

groundnut oil for deep-frying

For coating

2 tablespoons all-purpose flour

1 egg, beaten

1 ¾ cups dry white bread crumbs

Sweat the onion in about 2 tablespoons of the butter until translucent.

Blanch the almonds in salted boiling water for 2 minutes, then drain, and rub off the skins. While still warm, place in a blender and blend until almost a paste.

Scrape the almond paste into a bowl and mix in the remaining 3 tablespoons of butter, then beat in the eggs, one at a time. Stir in the flour, chopped apricots and parsley, and softened onion, and season to taste. Using two tablespoons, shape the mixture into quenelles and put into the refrigerator to firm up.

To serve: Roll the quenelles in flour, then in beaten egg, and finally in the bread crumbs. Heat the oil to 375°F and deep-fry the beignets until golden brown and crisp. Drain on paper towels and serve hot (be generous with the pepper when seasoning).

Wine suggestion:

Côte Rôtie 'La Turque' 1990, E Guigal

195

Braised veal sweetbreads with saffron, vegetable tagliatelle

Serves 4

2¼lb (4 pieces) veal sweetbreads
1 lemon
2 tablespoons olive oil
⅓ cup butter
all-purpose flour
salt and pepper
½ garlic clove, finely crushed
½ cup sweet white wine
a generous pinch of saffron strands
7fl oz heavy cream

For this recipe it is important to have sweetbreads from the heart as they are large and rounded; the ones from the throat are thin and do not hold together.

Place the sweetbreads in a bowl under slowly running cold water for 15 minutes to disgorge. Put them into a saucepan of cold salted water over high heat and bring to a boil, skim, and turn down the heat to a gentle simmer for 10 minutes. Rinse under cold running water until cool enough to handle. Using a small sharp knife, cut away the fat and gristle, peel off the membrane, and form into even rounded shapes.

Pare the lemon rind and cut into thin julienne. Place in cold water and bring to a boil, drain, and refresh in ice-cold water. Repeat three times, then set aside.

Heat the oil and butter in a thick-bottomed saucepan until foaming. Roll the sweetbreads in seasoned flour, then cook in the oil and butter over medium heat for 20–25 minutes, basting and turning them occasionally, until golden all over.

Tip out the fat and add the garlic, wine, lemon juice, and saffron; simmer for 5 minutes, then add the cream. Bring back to a simmer, cover with wax paper, and cook for a further 15 minutes. Check for seasoning, then serve in warmed deep plates, sprinkled with the lemon rind.

Vegetable tagliatelle

peeled carrots
washed leeks and zucchini
butter
salt and pepper

Cut the vegetables into long thin strips to resemble tagliatelle. Blanch separately in salted boiling water, refresh and drain well. Reheat in a little butter over medium-high heat, season, and serve. These can also be mixed with pasta tagliatelle.

Baked potato
with creamed morel mushrooms

Serves 8 as a side dish;
4 as a light meal

1 ¼ cups dried morel mushrooms
8 baking potatoes
⅓ cup butter
1 bunch of chives
½ bunch of chervil
salt and pepper
2 shallots, finely chopped
1 ½ tablespoons Madeira
1 cup heavy cream
1 ¼ cups Emmental cheese, grated

Ideal as an accompaniment to roast red meat, or serve as a main course with a mixed leaf salad.

Soak the morels for an hour. Wash the potatoes and bake in a hot oven, 425°F, until tender.

When the potatoes are cooked, slice off the top third of each potato horizontally, and scoop out some of the potato into a bowl. Mash with a fork, adding 3 tablespoons of butter, the coarsely chopped herbs, salt, and pepper; keep warm.

Drain the morels, cut into thin slices, and wash well to remove any grit. Sweat the shallots with the remaining 2 tablespoons of butter, then add the morels, and continue cooking for 3 minutes. Deglaze with the Madeira, and when completely evaporated, add the cream, season to taste, and reduce to a thick sauce consistency.

Spoon the morel mixture into the potato boats, then cover with the mashed potato and top with grated cheese. Return to the hot oven until piping hot and lightly glazed.

Le trou Gascon (Armagnac sorbet)

Serves 8

3 cups water
2¼ cups granulated sugar
1½oz glucose
1 cup dry white wine
1 cup Armagnac

This can be served between a fish and meat main course to cleanse the palate and refresh the appetite. Or serve as a dessert with fresh grapes that have been peeled and steeped in a little Armagnac.

First make a stock syrup with 2 cups of the water, the granulated sugar, and glucose. Bring to a boil, stirring occasionally to dissolve the sugar, and boil for 3 minutes. Add the remaining water, wine, and Armagnac to a boiling syrup, then remove from the heat, cover, and let cool.

When cold, churn in an ice-cream maker until frozen; serve immediately.

A man of many talents, Peter Ustinov delighted us with this droll self-portrait

Roast figs with honey and pistachios

Serves 6

18 purple figs
⅓ cup unsalted butter
ground cinnamon and ginger
1 cup flower-scented clear honey
juice of 2 lemons
1 cup peeled pistachios, chopped

Cut the stems off the figs, then cut a cross to about half way through the fruit. Open up slightly to reveal the speckled red flesh. Put a small pat of butter in each fig and place in a roasting pan, dust with a little cinnamon and ginger, then drizzle with some of the honey. This can be done in advance.

To serve: Heat the oven to 425°F. Roast the figs until the tips have caramelized, 8–10 minutes.

Put three figs on each plate. Place the roasting pan over medium-high heat and pour in the remaining honey; cook until syrupy, stirring all the time. Add the the lemon juice and mix well. Pass through a fine sieve and spoon a little over each fig; sprinkle the chopped pistachios over the figs. Great as it is but even better with pistachio ice cream (page 252).

Wine suggestion:
Vouvray 'Clos du Bourg' Moelleux
1990, S A Huet

Vanilla crème brulée with almond puff pastry sticks

Serves 4

1 cup heavy cream
⅓ cup whole milk
1 vanilla bean, scraped
4 egg yolks
3 tablespoons caster sugar, plus
3–4 tablespoons for the topping
2 teaspoons vanilla extract

You can use any ramekin dishes for this, but I like to use large shallow ones, for a higher proportion of crunchy brûlée to rich cream. Demerara sugar gives a crunchier topping, but does not stay that way for long.

Heat the oven to 275°F. Put the cream, milk, and vanilla bean into a saucepan and heat to boiling point. Cover and let infuse for 10 minutes.

Whisk the yolks and 3 tablespoons of the sugar together until pale and thick, add the vanilla extract and pour the boiling cream on to the mixture; stir well, then pour into four ramekins. Cook in a water bath in the oven until just set, about 20 minutes. Let cool.

Sprinkle with a thin, even layer of sugar, and caramelize with a blowtorch or under a very hot broiler. Repeat several times until you have the desired degree of golden brown crackling topping. Let cool; serve within 2 hours.

Sacristains

Heat the oven to 375°F. Roll out a sheet of puff pastry to ⅛in thickness, brush with beaten egg, and sprinkle with finely chopped almonds. Using a long sharp knife, cut strips of pastry ½in wide and 4in long. Twist five times and place on a baking sheet. Cook until golden and crisp, dust with confectioner's sugar, and serve warm with the crème brulée.

Compotes of three plums with Breton shortbread

Serves 4

3 cups dessert wine
⅔ cup caster sugar
4 vanilla beans, split
10oz of each variety of plum:
Victoria, greengage, and damson

At the end of September, British plums are at their best. Victoria, greengage and damsons are three of my favorite varieties and this recipe uses all three, served with rich shortbread biscuits and a generous spoonful of crème fraîche.

Bring the wine to a boil with the sugar and split vanilla beans. Divide this syrup between three saucepans to cook each type of plum separately. The plums should not be covered with liquid as they will render their own juices. You may need to add more sugar if the plums are a little sour. Cover the plums with wax paper and simmer gently, turning them over carefully with a spoon after about 5 minutes. Cooking time will depend on the ripeness and size of the plums: They are cooked when the skin is just breaking. Serve just warm with the Breton shortbread.

Breton shortbread

2¼ cups all-purpose flour
pinch of salt
1 cup unsalted butter, cubed—at room temperature
½ cup caster sugar
2 egg yolks
1 tablespoon crème fraîche
2 teaspoons vanilla extract
beaten egg, for brushing

Sift the flour and salt on to a clean work surface. Make a well in the center and add the butter, sugar, yolks, cream, and vanilla, then, using your fingertips, bring the central ingredients together without overworking. Gradually draw in the flour, again using your fingertips with delicate movements. Lightly bring together to form a thick sausage shape, cover with plastic wrap, and refrigerate for at least 2 hours.

Heat the oven to 350°F. On a very lightly floured work surface, roll out the dough to ¼in thick. Cut out 1½in diameter rounds, brush with beaten egg, and decorate with a fork. Cook on a wax paper-lined baking sheet for 15–18 minutes, until pale golden. Leave on the baking sheet to cool slightly before transferring to a wire rack to cool completely.

202

Omelet Rothschild

Serves 6–8

1 cup milk
3 egg yolks
4 tablespoons caster sugar
⅓ cup all-purpose flour
1 jigger of Cointreau
8 egg whites

For the apricots
1 cup water
⅔ cup caster sugar
1 vanilla bean, split
20 dried apricots
2 jiggers of Cointreau

For the apricots, boil the water and sugar with the vanilla bean, pour over the apricots, add a measure of Cointreau, and let macerate overnight.

Remove 12 apricots and a little of the syrup and reserve for the garnish. Purée the remaining apricots with a jigger of Cointreau to make a light sauce; if too thick, add a little of the syrup from the apricots.

Heat the oven to 350°F.

Heat the milk to boiling point. Whisk the yolks with 3 tablespoons of the sugar until pale and creamy, whisk in the flour and pour on the boiling milk. Return to the saucepan and bring back to a boil, stirring continuously. Remove from the heat, transfer to a large bowl, and stir in a jigger of Cointreau. Keep warm.

Heat four blini pans (4½in diameter) over medium heat. Whisk the egg whites with 1 tablespoon of caster sugar until soft peaks form. Stir half into the egg yolk mixture until evenly blended, then lightly fold in the rest. Butter the blini pans and spoon in the mixture. Cook in the oven for 6 minutes, then invert on to warmed plates and serve immediately, with the marinated apricots and the hot sauce.

Wine suggestion:
Château Suduiraut 1983 (Sauternes)

Waffles with poached pear, bitter chocolate sauce, and Poire Williams cold sabayon

Serves 4

Poached pears

2 cups water

1½ cups caster sugar

1 vanilla bean, split

4 ripe Comice or Williams pears

Put the water, sugar, and vanilla bean into a small saucepan just large enough to hold the pears and bring to simmering point. Peel the pears, leaving a band of peel around the stalks. Using the point of a small knife, cut around the edges of the peel to make a frilly collar. Remove the core from the bottom of the pear and then place in the simmering syrup and cover with wax paper. The cooking time depends on the ripeness and variety of the pear; a knife or needle should easily pierce the pear when cooked. Let cool slightly in the syrup.

Creme légère Poire Williams

3 eggs
3 egg yolks
¾ cup caster sugar
3 sheets of gelatin
7 fl oz eau de vie de Poire Williams
1 quart heavy cream

Whisk the eggs, yolks, and sugar in an electric food mixer for 12 minutes, until the mixture is very pale and foamy. Soften the gelatin in cold water, then squeeze out excess water. Warm the pear brandy and melt the gelatin in it. Pour this into the egg mixture and whisk well. Whisk the cream until soft peaks form and gently incorporate into the egg mixture. Refrigerate for at least 3 hours before serving.

Waffles

2¼ cups all-purpose flour
1 pinch of salt
3 tablespoons caster sugar
3 eggs, separated
1¼ cups milk
⅓ cup butter, melted
1 teaspoon vanilla extract
confectioner's sugar for dusting

Sift the flour and salt into a large bowl, add the sugar and egg yolks, and whisk together while gradually pouring in the milk. Stir in the melted butter and vanilla extract. Cover and let rest at room temperature for at least 2 hours.

To serve: Whisk the egg whites to form firm peaks, fold into the yolk mixture, and cook in a generously buttered hot waffle maker, to make 8–10 waffles.

Bitter chocolate sauce

½ cup unsweetened cocoa powder
confectioner's sugar
1 cup water
2 tablespoons butter, cut into small pieces

Put the cocoa and sugar in a saucepan with the water and bring to a boil, whisking well. Add the butter and bring back to a boil, whisking continuously.

To assemble: Using a sharp knife, slice each pear several times lengthwise, keeping the stem end intact. Place a pear on each plate and press lightly to make a fan shape. Add a freshly cooked waffle and a big scoop of Poire Williams mousse. Dust with confectioner's sugar and drizzle with bitter chocolate sauce.

Omelet soufflé with prunes and Armagnac

Serves 6

24 prunes, pitted
7fl oz Armagnac
4 tablespoons caster sugar
8 egg whites
confectioner's sugar for dusting

Marinate the prunes in the Armagnac with 3 tablespoons of the sugar for at least a week in an airtight container.

Press six of the prunes through a fine sieve and add to the crème patissière. Heat the oven to 350°F.

Beat the egg whites until frothy, then add 1 tablespoon of sugar and continue to whisk until stiff. Stir one-third of the whites into the crème patissière, then lightly fold in the rest. Divide this mixture between six hot buttered blini pans (4½in diameter) and cook over medium heat for 15 seconds, then place in the oven for 6–8 minutes.

Invert on to warmed plates and decorate with three marinated prunes per person, warmed in some of their marinade. Dust with confectioner's sugar and serve with warm crème anglaise flavored with some of the marinade.

Creme patissière

1 cup milk
3 egg yolks
3 tablespoons caster sugar
⅓ cup all-purpose flour

Heat the milk to boiling point. Whisk the yolks with the sugar until pale and creamy, whisk in the flour, and pour the boiling milk on to the mixture. Return to the saucepan and bring back to a boil, stirring continuously. Remove from the heat and transfer to a large bowl.

Harlequin chocolate mousse

Serves 12

2 eggs
1 sheet of gelatin
⅓ cup Grand Marnier
14oz white chocolate
2 cups whipping cream

White chocolate mousse

Put the eggs in a stainless steel or glass bowl and place the bowl over a saucepan of simmering water. Soften the gelatin in cold water, then squeeze out excess water. Warm the Grand Marnier and melt the gelatin in it. Add to the eggs and whisk continuously until the eggs are foamy and form soft peaks; the eggs should be just warm to the touch—be careful not to overcook or the eggs will scramble. Remove from the double boiler and let cool slightly.

Melt the chocolate. Whip the cream until firm but not too stiff. Fold the chocolate into the egg mixture, followed by the whipped cream.

Dark chocolate mousse

Make as for the white chocolate mousse, replacing the Grand Marnier with dark rum and the white chocolate with 10oz unsweetened chocolate (70% cocoa solids).

To assemble: Place alternate spoonfuls of white and dark chocolate mousse into 12 individual molds or a large bowl. Chill for at least 3 hours.

To serve: Invert—or scoop out—the mousse and decorate with a chocolate, almond, and orange crisp.

Chocolate, almond, and orange crisps

7oz chocolate couverture
(64% cocoa solids)
¼ cup nibbed almonds, toasted
finely grated zest of ½ an orange

Melt the chocolate and stir in the almonds and orange zest. Using a palette knife, spread the chocolate on wax paper, cover with another sheet and, using a rolling pin, roll out until very thin. Chill in the refrigerator until almost set, then cut out the desired shapes.

Apples Brussels sprouts

Oranges Oyst.

Scallop.

Winter

Cardoons Clementines Hare
s Parsnips Pheasant Salsify
Swede Teal Venison Woodcock

Creamy lentil and pheasant soup

Serves 6

⅔ cup Puy lentils

5 strips smoked bacon

1 carrot

1 small onion

1 garlic clove

1 bouquet garni

5 cups game stock (page 265)

salt and pepper

½ cup light cream

Rinse the lentils in cold water. Drain and place in a saucepan with the bacon, peeled vegetables, garlic, bouquet garni, and stock. Bring to a simmer and cook for 35 minutes, skimming occasionally, until the lentils are cooked.

Take out 2 tablespoons of lentils and set aside for the garnish. Continue cooking the rest of the lentils for another 10 minutes, then remove the bacon, bouquet garni, and carrot. Season well with salt and pepper, then pour the lentils and stock into a blender and blend until smooth.

Pass through a fine sieve into a clean saucepan. Add the cream and bring back to a boil; for a cappuccino effect, froth with a hand blender. Spoon the reserved lentils into six warmed soup bowls, pour in the hot soup, and place a quenelle of pheasant mousse in the soup.

Pheasant mousse

1 pheasant breast (about ¼lb)

1 egg white

1 cup double cream

salt and white pepper

about 1 quart chicken stock (page 264)

Remove the skin from the pheasant. Blend the pheasant meat in a blender with the egg white until smooth, then press through a fine sieve into a bowl set over ice. Using a rubber spatula, work in the cream a little at a time. Season with salt and a little white pepper. Cover and chill for at least 1 hour.

Heat the stock in a wide pan (the stock should be no deeper than 1in). Using two tablespoons dipped in cold water, shape the mousse into six quenelles. Drop these into the simmering stock and poach for 5 minutes. Delicately turn the quenelles and cook for a further 2 minutes. These can be kept warm in the stock, lightly covered with wax paper, for 20 minutes.

Onion soup with cider and Calvados

Serves 6

3lb French onions
1 tablespoon vegetable oil
3 tablespoons butter
¼ cup all-purpose flour
3 cups dry hard cider
1 bouquet garni
2½ quarts beef stock (page 265)
salt and pepper
sherry vinegar (optional)
6 egg yolks
3 tablespoons crème fraîche
6 tablespoons Calvados
1 country-style baguette
1 cup grated Gruyère

It is most important that the onions are of top quality, firm, and strong in taste. My favorites are a pink-fleshed French variety from Roscoff. You will need heatproof porcelain or earthenware dishes for this, as it is finished under the broiler.

Cut the onions in half, slice thinly, and place in a large, thick-bottomed saucepan with the oil and one-third of the butter. Cook over high heat, stirring occasionally, until the onions start to caramelize. Turn the heat down and continue cooking until the onions are soft but still in slices, about 20–30 minutes.

Meanwhile, make a brown roux by melting the remaining butter in a large, thick-bottomed saucepan. Add the flour and stir well over medium heat until light brown and nutty smelling. Pour two-thirds of the cider into the pan in a slow stream, whisking vigorously to prevent any lumps from forming. Add the bouquet garni and bring to a boil. Add the stock and simmer for 30 minutes, skimming occasionally.

When the onions are soft, pour the remaining cider over them, and bring to a boil. Strain the thickened stock over the onions, stir, and season well with salt and pepper. Simmer for 15 minutes before serving.

To serve: For a slightly sweet and sour taste, add a few drops of sherry vinegar to the soup. In each soup dish, lightly beat an egg yolk with ½ tablespoon crème fraîche and 1 tablespoon Calvados. Pour the piping hot soup on to this mixture, stirring continuously. Place two or three slices of toasted baguette on the soup and top with a generous handful of grated Gruyère. Place under a hot broiler until the cheese begins to bubble, then serve immediately.

Lobster bisque flavored with Armagnac

Serves 10–12

6½–7lb lobster heads
(see page 267)
1 large onion, chopped
1 carrot, chopped
2 celery stalks, chopped
2 tablespoons olive oil
4 sprigs of parsley stalks
1 sprig of thyme
1 bay leaf
2 large tomatoes
2 tablespoons tomato paste
½ teaspoon cayenne pepper,
plus extra, to serve
1 tablespoon brandy
1¼ cups dry white wine
2 quarts fish stock (page 266)
1 quart veal stock (page 264)
sea salt
2 cups heavy cream
about ½ cup Armagnac

This classic soup never fails to impress. The richness can be varied by how much the lobster stock is reduced and by the amount of cream added.

Crush the lobster heads with a mallet or a rolling pin until they are well broken up. Sweat the onion, carrot, and celery with the olive oil in a large saucepan. When the vegetables are lightly browned, add the herbs and lobster heads, stirring so nothing sticks or burns. After about 5 minutes, when the bones are hot, stir in the tomatoes, tomato paste, and cayenne pepper. Pour in the brandy and stir well for a minute or two, then add the wine, and boil for at least 3 minutes.

Add the stocks and bring to a boil; season lightly with sea salt. Simmer for 40 minutes, stirring occasionally and skimming off the scum that appears on the surface.

Drain through a colander set over a large bowl, pressing the bones well to extract all the juices and flavor. Then pass this liquid through a fine sieve into a clean saucepan. Bring to a boil and skim.

To serve: Bring to a boil and reduce by one-third. Add up to 2 cups heavy cream, according to taste, and boil for 5 minutes. For a cappuccino effect, froth with a hand blender, then pour into warmed soup bowls, to which you have added a little Armagnac (I suggest about 2 teaspoons per person). If you have any lobster claw meat left over from another recipe, add that too. Sprinkle with cayenne pepper and serve immediately.

Scallops baked in their shell, flavored with ginger

Serves 6

12 large scallops (white meat only)

1 large carrot

1 leek (white and yellow parts only)

1 tablespoon ginger confit

(page 62)

2 tablespoons light soy sauce

1 tablespoon light sesame oil

juice of 1 lime

salt and pepper

10oz puff pastry (page 278—

trimmings can be used)

1 egg, beaten

To serve (optional)

beurre blanc (page 270)

fresh ginger juice (page 287)

Always insist on diver-caught scallops, as the dredged ones are likely to be full of sand and are also not very environmentally friendly, as the sea bed is damaged by dredging. It's best to buy scallops in their shells—making absolutely sure they are alive—but if you buy them already cleaned, specify unsoaked meat. Scallop flesh can absorb 10 per cent of its own weight in water; you pay for this water and it does nothing to enhance the flavor or texture of the scallop. For this recipe you need both top and bottom shells, so ask your fishmonger to set some aside for you; the best size is about 4½in at the widest part. Clean them well before you start the recipe.

Heat the oven to 375°F. Cut the carrot and leek into fine julienne; wash the leek julienne well. Blanch both julienne in boiling salted water for 20 seconds, refresh in ice-cold water, drain, and dry well. Add the ginger confit with 2 teaspoons of its syrup, and toss with the soy sauce, sesame oil, and lime juice.

Place a small pile of the vegetable julienne in the center of the deep scallop shells. Slice the scallops horizontally into thin discs and arrange in the shells in an overlapping flower pattern. Put the remaining julienne on top of the scallops and divide any remaining liquid between the shells. Sprinkle lightly with salt and generously with pepper.

Cover with the top shell and seal with a strip of rolled out puff pastry dough, making sure there are no gaps. Brush the pastry lightly with beaten egg. Place the shells on a bed of rock salt to keep them flat and cook in a preheated oven for 9 minutes. Serve immediately, opening the shells at table to enjoy the aromas as they are released. This can be served with a beurre blanc flavored with a little fresh ginger juice.

214

Poached scallops with leeks and smoked salmon

Serves 6

*6 very large scallops (about
2½oz each)*
1 large leek
3 tablespoons Chardonnay wine
salt and pepper
½ cup heavy cream
½ cup unsalted butter, cubed
juice of 1 lemon
*grated zest of ½ an unwaxed
lemon*
*3 thin slices of smoked salmon, cut
into very thin strips*
caviar to garnish (optional)

It can be difficult to find really large scallops because of overfishing, but you can use 12 or 18 smaller scallops if the big ones are not available. If you feel confident enough to prepare them yourself, buy them in the shell, ensuring they are alive. As for the previous recipe, scallops should always be diver caught, not dredged, and should be fresh, not soaked in water to increase their weight.

Remove the outside leaf of the leek and set aside. Cut the white, yellow, and tender green parts into 2½in x ½in strips. Blanch in boiling salted water until cooked but still a little crunchy, refresh in ice-cold water and drain well.

Chop the outer green leaf of the leek and place in a saucepan with all the leek trimmings. Add ⅔ cup of water and boil for 5 minutes to make a leek stock. Pass through a fine sieve and set aside.

Put the scallops and wine into a wide saucepan over medium heat, season lightly, and bring to a simmer. Add enough of the leek stock to come three-quarters of the way up the scallops, turn the scallops, and continue to cook for no more than 2 minutes. For my taste, scallops are best cooked rare, otherwise they lose their flavor and delicate texture.

Remove the scallops from the pan and set aside. Turn up the heat to high, add the cream, and then whisk in the butter. Add the leeks to reheat in the sauce, together with the lemon juice and zest. Serve the leek ribbons and scallops in warmed deep plates with the strips of smoked salmon on top. If you are feeling extravagant—and I recommend it—a generous spoonful of sevruga caviar finishes the dish perfectly.

Chilled oysters with caviar

Serves 4

1 cucumber, cut into thin julienne

2 slices of smoked salmon, cut into

thin julienne

2 shallots, finely chopped

12 sprigs of dill, chopped

1 ½ cups crème fraîche

salt and pepper

juice of 1 lemon

12 flat native oysters

12 Pacific oysters

8 tablespoons oscietre caviar

Gently mix the julienne of cucumber and smoked salmon with the shallots and dill. Season the crème fraîche with salt and pepper, and add just enough of the crème fraîche to bind the cucumber mixture. Add a little lemon juice, to taste.

Open the oysters and clean the deep half shells. Place the shells on four oyster plates and fill with the cucumber and salmon mixture.

Place the oysters back in their shells and add a teaspoon of caviar to each. Serve immediately.

For an alternative presentation, or if you don't have any oyster plates, serve the oysters on a bed of very fine julienne of carrots, leeks and beetroot.

Glazed oysters on a bed of sauerkraut with smoked bacon

Serves 6

10oz piece of smoked Alsace bacon
(very heavily smoked)
36 medium-large rock oysters
3 tablespoons dry white wine
1 ½ cups cooked sauerkraut
½ cup heavy cream
hollandaise sauce (page 270)
3 tablespoons whipping cream,
whipped until soft peaks form

This can be served in special oyster plates that have indentations in the shape of six oysters in one plate; alternatively, keep the bottom shell after opening the oysters; wash thoroughly, then place the shells on a little bed of rock salt to keep them stable.

Blanch the smoked bacon in boiling water for about 15 minutes, or until cooked. Drain and rinse under cold running water. Cut the bacon into very small lardons (half the length of a matchstick).

Open the oysters over a plate to collect the juices. Put the oysters and their juices into a saucepan with the wine, bring to a simmer, and cook for 20 seconds, then drain into a sieve set over another saucepan to collect the liquid.

Stir the lardons into the warmed sauerkraut and arrange in neat little piles on the oyster plates. Place an oyster on each pile of sauerkraut.

Bring the oyster liquid to a boil, add the heavy cream, and quickly reduce by half. Remove from the heat and whisk in the hollandaise sauce and whipped cream; spoon over the oysters and place under a very hot broiler until lightly browned. Serve immediately.

Wine suggestion:
Riesling 'Cuvée Frédéric Émile' 1995,
F E Trimbach

Duck pastilla with foie gras

Serves 4

1 duck leg confit (page 237)
4 sheets of pastilla/brique (North African paper-thin pancakes, similar to filo pastry)
oil for deep-frying
4 slices of fresh duck foie gras (3½oz each)
salt and pepper
ground cinnamon
confectioner's sugar

Shred the duck confit and divide between the four pancakes. Fold the pancakes into parcels, sealing the edges with a little water, then trim the excess pancake to make 2in x 1in rectangles. Deep-fry until crisp, then drain on paper towels; keep the parcels warm.

Heat a thick-bottomed frying pan over high heat, add the foie gras, and cook until brown on both sides, about 2 minutes; season with salt and pepper.

Cinnamon sauce

7fl oz full-bodied red wine
1 cinnamon stick
2 tablespoons sugar
1 tablespoon unsalted butter
sherry vinegar

Put the wine in a saucepan with the cinnamon stick and sugar, bring to a boil, and reduce until syrupy. Season with salt and pepper, remove the cinnamon stick, and whisk in the butter and a drop of sherry vinegar.

To assemble: Cut each pastilla in half and dust generously with ground cinnamon and confectioner's sugar. Place at the top of the warmed plates and place the foie gras beneath. Drizzle the sauce around the plate and serve immediately.

Foie gras terrine marbled with celeriac and lentils

Serves 12–16

2¼lb duck or goose fat

14oz celeriac, peeled and cut into
¾in x 3in strips

⅔ cup Puy lentils, soaked
overnight

salt and freshly ground pepper

2 whole fresh duck foie gras
(about 14oz each)

4 shallots, chopped

2 tablespoons brandy

4 sheets of gelatin

3 sprigs of parsley, chopped

Put the fat in a thick-bottomed saucepan over low heat, add the celeriac, and cook at a very gentle simmer for 30 minutes or until tender. Drain and keep the fat for another use.

Rinse the lentils and place in a saucepan, cover with water, and bring to a boil. Simmer for 25 minutes or until tender. Season with salt, let rest for 5 minutes, and then drain until completely dry.

Divide the foie gras into their natural two lobes, scrape off any green parts, and then cut the larger lobe lengthwise into four slices and the smaller lobe into two slices; season with salt and pepper. Heat a thick-bottomed frying pan over high heat and cook the foie gras (you will have to do this in batches) until well browned, then turn and brown the other side; it should remain soft to the touch and pink inside. Drain and reserve the fat. Repeat until all the foie gras is cooked.

Take 7fl oz of the foie gras fat and sweat the shallots in this. When they are cooked, add the lentils and brandy, bring to a boil and then immediately remove from the heat.

Soak the gelatin in a little water to soften, then squeeze dry, and add to the lentils together with the parsley. Taste and adjust the seasoning.

To assemble: Line a terrine (12in x 4in x 4in) with several layers of plastic wrap, letting it overlap at the sides. Fill the terrine with layers of celeriac, foie gras, and lentils. Cover with the overlapping plastic wrap and place a weight on top—7lb should be enough. Refrigerate overnight; some fat and juices will overflow.

Slice and serve with toasted country-style bread.

Soufflé suissesse

Serves 4

3 tablespoons butter
6 tablespoons all-purpose flour
2 cups milk
5 egg yolks
salt and freshly ground white pepper
6 egg whites
2½ cups heavy cream
1¾ cups Gruyère or Emmental cheese, grated

Heat the oven to 400°F.

Melt the butter in a thick-bottomed saucepan, whisk in the flour and cook, stirring continuously, for about 1 minute. Whisk in the milk and boil for 3 minutes, whisking all the time to prevent any lumps from forming. Beat in the yolks and remove from the heat; season with salt and pepper. Cover with a piece of buttered wax paper to prevent a skin from forming.

Whisk the egg whites with a pinch of salt until they form firm, not stiff, peaks. Add a third of the egg whites to the yolk mixture and beat with a whisk until evenly mixed, then gently fold in the remaining egg whites. Spoon the mixture into four well-buttered 3in diameter tartlet molds and place in the oven for 3 minutes, until the tops begin to turn golden.

Meanwhile, season the cream with a little salt, warm it gently, and pour into a gratin dish. Invert the soufflés into the cream, sprinkle the grated cheese over the soufflés, then return to the oven for 5 minutes. Serve immediately.

Lobster soufflé with quail's egg and brandy

Serves 8

2 tablespoons butter

¼ cup all-purpose flour

1 cup lobster stock (page 267)

2 egg yolks

salt and cayenne pepper

8 egg whites

8 quail's eggs, boiled for 1 minute

1 boiled lobster, cut into small pieces

lobster bisque (page 212)

1–2 tablespoons brandy

2 tablespoons each of grated Gruyère, Emmental, and mature Cheddar cheese

Melt the butter in a thick-bottomed saucepan, whisk in the flour and cook, stirring continuously, for about 1 minute. Whisk in the lobster stock and boil for 1 minute, whisking all the time to prevent any lumps from forming. Beat in the egg yolks and remove from the heat; season with salt and cayenne pepper. Cover with a piece of buttered wax paper and let cool.

Heat the oven to 425°F. Whisk the egg whites with a pinch of salt until they form soft peaks. Add a third of the egg whites to the lobster béchamel and beat with a whisk until evenly mixed, then gently fold in the remaining egg whites. Spoon the mixture into well-buttered 3in diameter tartlet molds until half full, then add a soft-boiled quail's egg and a few pieces of lobster meat to each mold. Cover with the remaining soufflé mixture and cook in the hot oven for 5 minutes.

Bring the bisque to a boil and add a dash of brandy; pour into eight warmed heatproof soup plates. Invert the soufflés on to the bisque, sprinkle the grated cheese over the soufflés, then place under a hot broiler to glaze. Serve immediately.

Wine suggestion:
Chablis St Martin 1998,
Domaine Laroche

222

Turbot spiked with smoked salmon, buttered cabbage with sage

Serves 6

½lb smoked salmon (not sliced)

6 pieces of turbot (6oz each), taken from a big fish so that each piece is about ¾in thick

3 shallots, chopped

olive oil

3½oz fish trimmings and bones (preferably turbot), rinsed

1 tablespoon white wine vinegar

1 bottle Riesling wine

⅔ cup butter, cubed

salt and pepper

Cut the smoked salmon into 36 sticks, 1in long and ⅛in thick. Using a small pointed knife or darning needle, make six evenly spaced incisions in each piece of turbot and insert the salmon sticks; they should protrude slightly.

Cook the shallots in a saucepan with a little oil and butter until deep brown and caramelized. Add the fish trimmings and sweat for 5–6 minutes, stirring frequently. Add the vinegar and wine, then simmer for 20 minutes, skimming frequently. Strain the sauce through a fine sieve into a clean saucepan, then boil until reduced by two-thirds.

Heat a large non-stick frying pan until very hot. Add a drop of olive oil and cook the turbot until crisp and browned, then turn and cook the other side; this should take no more than 2–3 minutes on each side. Remove from the pan and put on paper towels to rest for 3 minutes.

To serve: Place a bed of buttered cabbage on six warmed plates and put the fish on top. Whisk the butter into the hot sauce, season with salt and pepper, and pour around the fish. Serve immediately.

Buttered cabbage with sage

1 Savoy cabbage
1 carrot, diced
½ cup butter
salt and pepper
1 sprig of sage, leaves finely chopped

Discard the outer leaves of the cabbage, then cut the cabbage into quarters, remove the core and shred the leaves finely. Blanch in boiling salted water until tender but still a little crunchy. Refresh in ice-cold water and drain in a colander.

Sweat the carrot in a wide pan with half the butter. After 5 minutes add the cabbage and the remaining butter, salt, pepper, the finely chopped sage leaves, and 2 tablespoons of water. Place over very low heat, cover with wax paper, and cook for about 10 minutes, stirring occasionally. The cabbage should be very tender and coated in butter.

Sauerkraut of seafood

Serves 4

1 live lobster (about 1lb 6oz)

1 leek

½ onion, very thinly sliced

½ tablespoon duck or goose fat

½ tablespoon cumin seeds

2 tablespoons juniper berries

1¼ cups cooked sauerkraut

3 tablespoons dry white wine

3 tablespoons chicken stock
(page 264)

7fl oz beurre blanc (page 270)

1 tablespoon gin

12 mussels

4 baby squid

4 Venus clams

4 pieces of red mullet (1½oz each)

4 pieces of sea bass (1½oz each)

12 cooked langoustines

Kill the lobster, then boil in lightly salted water for 8 minutes. Remove the lobster; reserve the water. Cut the tail into four pieces; crack the claws to reveal the meat; crack the legs and remove the meat; reserve for the fish sausage, if making.

Cut the leek into large diamonds, wash and then blanch in boiling salted water, refresh in cold water and drain.

Sweat the onion with the duck fat until soft. Add the cumin seeds, together with half the juniper berries tied up in cheesecloth. Add the sauerkraut and mix well with a wooden spoon, then add the wine and boil for 3 minutes. Add the stock, cover with wax paper, and simmer for 20 minutes.

Bring the beurre blanc to a simmer, then remove from the heat and add the remaining crushed juniper berries and gin. Infuse for 2 minutes, strain, and reheat the leeks in the sauce.

Poach the uncooked seafood and fish in the lobster cooking water. Slice the fish sausage and steam over the fish. Drop in the lobster pieces and partly peeled langoustines for 10 seconds to reheat. Arrange the fish and seafood on a pile of hot sauerkraut and spoon over the beurre blanc. Serve immediately, with a side dish of boiled potatoes rolled in melted butter and chopped parsley.

Fish sausage

9oz whiting

1 egg white

⅔ cup heavy cream

1 tablespoon chopped fresh herbs,
such as chives, dill, tarragon

salt and pepper

lobster meat from the legs

Purée the fish and egg white in a blender. Push through a fine sieve into a bowl set over ice, beat in the cream, herbs, salt, and pepper, and mix in small pieces of lobster meat. Place on a double layer of plastic wrap and roll into a sausage shape. Tie both ends with string, and tie four pieces of string along the length to keep its shape. Poach in simmering salted water for 15 minutes, turning frequently. Let cool in the water until tepid, then refrigerate.

Roast fillet of sea bass, parsnip purée, and caramelized garlic

Serves 4

2 sea bass (1lb 6oz each)

olive oil

3 shallots, sliced

⅔ cup button mushrooms, sliced

1 tablespoon white wine vinegar

½ cup dry white wine

1½ cups veal stock (page 264)

salt and pepper

1 tablespoon butter

Scale and fillet the sea bass, remove the pin bones using a pair of tweezers, rinse the fish and dry with paper towel. Score the skin of the fish several times with a sharp knife; this will help to prevent the fish from curling during cooking. Leave the bones (not the heads) to soak in cold water.

To make the sauce, heat a little olive oil in a saucepan and cook the shallots for about 5 minutes, until golden and soft. Add the mushrooms and continue to cook for 10 minutes, stirring occasionally. Drain the fish bones, add to the pan, and cook for 5–6 minutes. Add the vinegar and wine and let the wine come to a boil for 3 minutes, then add the stock, season lightly, and simmer for 30 minutes, skimming at regular intervals. Pass through a fine sieve into a clean saucepan, bring back to a boil, and whisk in the butter to thicken and gloss the sauce.

Heat a non-stick frying pan until smoking hot, add a few drops of olive oil, then add the fish, skin down, season with salt and pepper, and press the fish down with a palette knife if it begins to curl up. Once the skin is well browned, turn the fillets over and cook the other side; the whole process should not take more than 5–6 minutes, depending on the thickness of the fish.

To serve: Spoon the parsnip purée on to warmed plates, make a hollow in the center, and fill with the caramelized garlic and shallots. Pour the sauce around the purée, place the fish on top, and add a few parsnip crisps for decoration.

Caramelized garlic

8 small shallots
20 garlic cloves
olive oil

Peel the shallots and garlic. Blanch the shallots in boiling salted water for 10 minutes or until tender—cut them in half if large—then drain well. Put the garlic in a small saucepan of boiling salted water, bring to a boil for 2 minutes, then drain and change the water; repeat four times; drain well. Heat a little olive oil in a frying pan over medium heat, add the shallots and garlic and cook, shaking the pan so they don't stick, until caramelized.

Parsnip purée

5 parsnips
½ cup milk
1 tablespoon butter
salt and pepper

Peel the parsnips and cut them into big chunks. Cook in boiling salted water until tender. Bring the milk to a boil and set aside. Drain the parsnips well, then put in a blender with the butter and some of the boiled milk and blend until totally smooth: The purée should be the consistency of heavy cream, so add more milk if necessary. Season and keep warm.

Parsnip crisps

1 parsnip
oil for deep-frying

Peel the parsnip and slice lengthwise, using a mandolin to slice it as thinly as possible. Deep-fry in hot oil until crisp. Drain on paper towels to absorb any excess fat and set aside in a dry place.

Steamed lobster wrapped in spinach

Serves 4

2 live lobsters (1lb 2oz each)
4 very large spinach leaves
olive oil
salt and pepper
4 sage leaves
9oz small girolles
½ cup butter, cut into small pieces
1 shallot, finely chopped
¼ cup dry white wine
⅔ cup chicken stock (page 264)
1 tablespoon heavy cream
12 dried tomato halves
(page 273)

Kill the lobsters and cut in half with a heavy knife. Remove and discard the intestine and sand bag found in the head. Scoop out the body flesh with a spoon and set aside. Remove the claws and cook in boiling salted water for 3 minutes, then crack and extract the meat.

Blanch the spinach leaves in boiling salted water, taking care not to damage them, refresh in ice-cold water and pat dry with paper towels. Lightly brush four large sheets of plastic wrap with olive oil to prevent sticking and lay out the spinach leaves. On each leaf, place the flesh of half a lobster, season lightly with salt and pepper, fold over the spinach leaf and then the plastic wrap to form a ball. Place in a steamer with the sage stalks and cook for 9–11 minutes.

Clean the girolles carefully and wash if necessary. Put a knob of butter in a sauté pan and, when it is foaming, add the shallot; cook for 1 minute to soften the shallot, then add the girolles, season with salt and pepper, and cook for 2 minutes, stirring occasionally. Add the wine and increase the heat to reduce the liquid by two-thirds, then add the chicken stock and reduce by two-thirds. Stir in the cream and the pieces of butter to emulsify the sauce. Finally, stir in the dried tomatoes and the sage leaves, cut into very thin julienne.

Pour the sauce into warmed soup plates; remove the plastic wrap from the lobster parcels, and place one in each plate.

Whole roast baby turbot with scallops, prawns, and herb butter

Serves 4

1 small turbot (4lb)
salt and pepper
olive oil
3 tablespoons butter
4 small scallops (white meat only),
sliced in half horizontally
3½ oz peeled small prawns
(crevettes grises)
1 lemon, cut into 8 segments
4 scallions, thinly sliced
1 tablespoon each of roughly
chopped flat-leaf parsley, chervil,
tarragon

1lb 2oz white potatoes
½ cup milk
4 tablespoons strong flavored
extra virgin olive oil
3 sprigs of flat-leaf parsley,
finely chopped
salt and white pepper

Heat the oven to 425°F. Remove the gills from the turbot and gut through the head rather than through the side. Using a pair of heavy-duty scissors, snip off the tail and fins; rinse the fish and dry thoroughly. Season with salt and pepper. Drizzle a little olive oil in a hot flameproof oven dish, add the fish, and place in the hot oven for 12 minutes.

Take out of the oven and carefully transfer the fish to a serving platter, cover, and keep warm.

Put the same dish over high heat and add the butter; when it is foaming add the sliced scallops; toss them in the butter for 20 seconds, then add the prawns and toss for 10 seconds. Finally, put the segments of lemon into the pan with the scallions and herbs. Pour over the turbot and serve with olive oil mashed potatoes.

Olive oil mashed potatoes

Peel and quarter the potatoes, place in salted water, and simmer until tender. Bring the milk to a boil and set aside.Drain the potatoes in a colander and leave for a couple of minutes to let the steam evaporate. Push through a potato ricer or coarse sieve, then gradually stir in the hot milk to achieve the desired consistency (you may not need to add all the milk, depending on the moisture in the potatoes). Stir in the olive oil and parsley, and season with salt and pepper. Serve with a little more olive oil drizzled over the top for a glossy finish.

Poached turbot in Bandol wine with bacon

Serves 6

2 red onions, roughly chopped

1 tablespoon caster sugar

2 bottles Bandol wine or similar,
deeply colored full-bodied red
wine, such as Syrah or Cabernet

1 leek

2 celery stalks

3 sticks of salsify

juice of 1 lemon

3 sprigs of flat-leaf parsley

9oz piece of smoked bacon

6 thin strips smoked bacon

½ cup heavy cream

1¼ cups butter

salt and pepper

red wine vinegar

6 pieces of turbot (6oz each)

Put the onions in a stainless steel or plastic container with the sugar and 1¼ bottles of the wine, cover, and marinate for 24 hours.

Trim the leek and wash under cold water, cut into 4½in x ½in strips, blanch in salted boiling water until cooked but still a little crunchy, then refresh in ice-cold water. Do the same with the celery. Scrub and peel the salsify, cook in boiling salted water with the juice of a lemon to keep them white; refresh in ice-cold water, drain, and then cut into the same size strips as the other vegetables. Blanch the parsley leaves, then mix with the vegetables.

Cut the piece of bacon into small lardons, place in a pan of cold water, and bring to a boil; drain, rinse, and dry on paper towels. Fry in a non-stick pan with a drop of olive oil until brown but not dry. Broil the bacon strips until crisp.

Put the marinade and onions in a saucepan and reduce until the liquid remaining just covers the onions. Add the cream, bring to a boil, and then whisk in 1 cup of the butter, cut into small cubes, a little at a time. Season with salt and pepper and keep warm, but do not boil. Finally, add a few drops of red wine vinegar to bring out the taste of the wine.

Put the remaining red wine in a wide pan with the turbot, season with salt, and bring to a boil; cover with a piece of wax paper and simmer for 30 seconds, then remove from the heat and let stand for 5 minutes.

Reheat the vegetables with the remaining butter. Drain the turbot and serve on a bed of buttered vegetables. Spoon the sauce over the fish and top with lardons and a strip of crisp broiled bacon.

Wine suggestion:
Bandol, Mas de la Rouvière 1995,
Domaine Bunan

Lobster cassoulet

Serves 4

1 cup small white navy beans
1 hind pig's foot
2 onions
2 carrots
2 garlic cloves
1 celery stalk
1 bouquet garni
7 strips thick-cut smoked bacon or
7oz dry-cured belly pork
1 tablespoon duck fat or olive oil
2 teaspoons tomato paste
4 large plum tomatoes, peeled,
deseeded, and chopped
1 quart chicken stock (page 264)
or lobster stock (page 267)
salt and pepper
4 Scottish lobsters (14oz–1lb
each)
1 teaspoon thyme leaves
1 tablespoon butter

The best, most authentic beans for cassoulet are Tarbais beans—from Tarbes in southwest France. Soak the beans overnight in plenty of water, drain, and rinse under cold running water.

Scrape and burn off any hair left on the pig's foot, boil in unsalted water for 45 minutes, then let cool in the water.

Peel all the vegetables. Add 1 onion, 1 carrot, and 1 garlic clove to the pan with the pig's foot. Add the celery, bouquet garni, belly pork, and beans, and top up with water if needed. Bring to a boil and skim, then simmer gently for about 45 minutes. Test to see if the beans are cooked; they should be tender but not burst open and, depending on the variety, they can take up to 1½ hours . Let cool in the cooking liquid.

Remove the pig's foot and pork and set aside. Remove the vegetables and bouquet garni and discard. Remove the bone from the pig's foot and dice the meat and skin, cut the pork into small lardons.

Slice the remaining onion and carrot, then sweat in the duck fat for 3 minutes. Add the tomato paste and remaining garlic, crushed, and cook, stirring, for a further 2 minutes. Add the chopped tomatoes, pig's foot, and pork, and drained beans. Add stock to cover, season with a little salt and plenty of pepper, and simmer for at least 30 minutes.

Kill the lobsters, then boil in court bouillon (page 266)or heavily salted water for 8 minutes. With a heavy knife, cut in half lengthwise, crack the claws and extract the meat.

Mix the thyme with the beans and spoon into deep, heatproof plates; add more stock to moisten if needed. Sit a half lobster on each plate, sprinkle some parsley and garlic bread crumbs on top, drizzle with a little melted butter, and place under a hot broiler until starting to turn golden.

Parsley and garlic bread crumbs

2 sprigs of curly parsley
6 slices of white bread, crusts cut
off, then dried in a low oven
3 garlic cloves, roughly chopped

Wash the parsley, pat dry, and chop roughly. Put the bread into a blender and blend to fine crumbs. Add the parsley and garlic and blend for a further 1 minute, until the crumbs have turned a fresh green color.

Coquelets braisés au vin rouge

Serves 6

3 small chickens (about 2lb each)
1 quart full-bodied red wine
14oz piece of smoked bacon
olive oil
1 onion, roughly chopped
1 carrot, roughly chopped
1 celery stalk, roughly chopped
1 garlic clove
1 bouquet garni
18 small button mushrooms, stalks trimmed and reserved
1 tablespoon all-purpose flour, toasted in the oven at 350°F until golden brown
1¼ cups port
5 cups veal stock (page 264)
salt and pepper
18 button onions
½ cup butter

Wine suggestion:
Arbin Mondeuse 'Vieilles Vignes' 1995
Louis Magnin

A variation on *coq au vin* using *coquelets*: Male chickens about 6 months old, traditionally available in fall and winter.

Cut each chicken in half lengthwise. Cut off the backbone and wing tips to leave six portions consisting of leg and breast. Put these in a stainless steel container, pour on just enough wine to cover, cover the container and refrigerate for 2–3 days.

Put the bacon in cold water and bring to a boil for 5 minutes; refresh and drain. Cut into lardons ¾in long x ½in thick, reserving the trimmings.

Drain the chicken and pat dry. Boil the marinade and skim well. In a large, thick-bottomed braising pan, sear the birds well in olive oil, then remove from the pan. Put the onion, carrot, celery, garlic, bouquet garni, mushroom stalks, and bacon trimmings into the pan and cook until caramelized. Add the toasted flour and stir for 3 minutes. Pour in the rest of the wine, the port, and marinade, and bring to a boil, stirring well until reduced by half. Return the chicken to the pan, add the stock, and bring to a simmer. Cover with wax paper and put in the oven at 275°F for 1 hour.

Fry the lardons in a little oil until golden but still moist; keep warm. Fry the mushrooms until lightly colored, season, and set aside. Fry the button onions gently in a little oil and butter until golden all round; drain and set aside.

Take out the chicken, cover, and keep warm. Pass the sauce through a fine sieve into a clean pan; skim well to remove any fat. Add the button onions and boil for 5 minutes. Add the mushrooms and simmer for a further 5 minutes. Whisk in the remaining butter and check the seasoning: It may need a pinch of sugar. Pour over the chickens and sprinkle the lardons on top. Serve piping hot with creamy mashed potato.

Confit de canard

6 duck legs (about 7oz each)
½ cup coarse sea salt
3–3½lb duck or goose fat
1 sprig of sage
1 sprig of rosemary

Confit is a much abused word. When talking about meat and poultry, I believe it should be used only for meats that are salted and then cooked slowly in plenty of fat; they can be preserved or eaten immediately, although it is generally agreed they improve if kept for at least a week. It is certainly not difficult to make your own confit. I usually use legs from Barbary ducks or *canards gras*—the ducks reared for foie gras.

Pork belly can also be made into confit. Be sure to use organic or free range pork as it makes the world of difference; my favorite breed for this is Middle White.

Place the duck legs in a single layer in a plastic, porcelain, or stainless steel tray. Sprinkle the salt over the duck legs and rub it in to the meat. Cover and refrigerate for 2 hours.

Melt the duck fat in a large saucepan over low heat. Brush the salt off the duck legs and pat dry with a cloth or paper towel. Carefully place in the fat with the herbs, cover with wax paper, and simmer gently until tender, about 1½ hours; do not let the fat boil. Let the duck cool in the fat.

To preserve, remove the herbs and pack the legs into an earthenware or glass dish or jar. Cover with the fat and refrigerate; this will keep for 6 weeks or more.

To serve: If using pork belly, cut it into cubes, scoring the skin. Reheat the duck or pork confit in the oven, then place under a hot broiler, skin side up, until crispy. Boil some small new potatoes, drain, and slice 1¼in thick. Fry in a little olive oil until golden, then add some finely chopped shallots, garlic, and parsley, and cook for a further minute. Serve the confit on top of the potatoes, together with curly endive salad dressed with olive oil and red wine vinegar.

Duck pot-au-feu with stuffed cabbage

Serves 4

2 leeks

4 carrots

6 large turnips

1 duck (Gressingham or Challans)

sea salt

1 quart chicken stock (page 264)

1 onion, peeled and quartered

2 celery stalks

1 sprig of thyme

2 cloves

15 pieces of star anise

1 tablespoon white peppercorns

Clarification

3 egg whites

1 shallot, finely chopped

¼ white part of leek, finely chopped

3½oz skinless chicken meat, finely chopped

10 star anise pods

6 parsley stalks

2 sprigs of tarragon

Cut the leeks into 2in lengths, rinse under cold water, and set aside. Trim the carrots into barrel shapes the same size as the leeks and discard the trimmings. Trim the turnips to the same size and keep the trimmings.

Prepare the duck by removing the wishbone and cutting off the wing tips at the joint; pull out any feathers that are left. Sprinkle a little salt in the cavity, then roll up the duck in cheesecloth; tie the ends tightly. Put the duck in a large saucepan with the stock, leek, and turnip trimmings, celery, onion, thyme, and spices. Add water to cover and bring to a boil. Skim and taste for seasoning, adding salt if required. Simmer very gently for 1 hour 10 minutes, then let cool in the stock.

Remove the duck and set aside. Skim all the fat from the stock, then strain the stock into a clean saucepan and remove 3½fl oz for the sauce Albert.

To clarify the stock, whisk all the clarification ingredients together until frothy, then pour into the duck stock. Stir constantly with a rubber spatula until it starts to boil, then turn the heat to very low. By this time there should be a crust of egg white at the surface; make a hole in the center of this to allow the stock to clarify properly. Simmer very gently for 20 minutes, then gently pass through cheesecloth. This consommé should be crystal clear.

To serve: Bring the consommé back to a boil and cook the leek, carrots, and turnips in this soup. When they are tender add the duck and reheat in the soup. Serve immediately, with the duck jus drizzled over the meat and the stuffed cabbage, sauce Albert and pear chutney (page 288) on the side.

Wine suggestion:
Clos St Denis 1993, Domaine Dujac

Stuffed cabbage

4 Savoy cabbage leaves
1 skinless, boneless chicken breast
(about 6oz)
1 egg white
7fl oz heavy cream
salt and pepper
6oz fresh duck foie gras
1 sprig of tarragon, chopped
1 sprig of parsley, chopped

Blanch the cabbage leaves in boiling salted water; drain, and refresh under cold running water.

Put the chicken and egg white in a blender and blend until smooth. Press through a fine sieve into a bowl. Set the bowl over ice and beat in the cream with a rubber spatula; season lightly with salt and pepper.

Cut the foie gras into ½in dice and cook in a very hot dry pan for 20 seconds. Drain and let cool.

Fold the foie gras and herbs into the chicken mousse. Divide this into four and spoon on to the cabbage leaves. Fold them into golfball-sized parcels, wrap tightly in plastic wrap, and steam for 12 minutes. Unwrap and serve with the duck.

Sauce Albert

½ onion, finely chopped
½ cup of the duck cooking stock
6 slices white bread, crusts removed
½ cup light cream
1 tablespoon grated horseradish
1 teaspoon English mustard

Put the onion in a saucepan, add the duck stock to cover, and boil for 5 minutes. Meanwhile, dice the bread. Add the cream to the pan with the onion and bring to a boil, then add the diced bread. Remove from the heat and beat in the horseradish and mustard.

Sweet and sour duck jus

1½ tablespoons caster sugar
1½ tablespoons white wine vinegar
13fl oz duck jus (page 268)
¼ cup unsalted butter

Melt the sugar and vinegar in a small saucepan and cook until light brown. Add the duck jus and reduce until syrupy, then whisk in the butter.

Braised lamb shanks in Madeira

Serves 6

6 lamb shanks
4lb lamb bones
1 onion, chopped
1 carrot, chopped
1 celery stalk, chopped
2 garlic cloves
1 bouquet garni
3 quarts chicken stock (page 264)
1 teaspoon white peppercorns
sea salt

Shanks of lamb have made a huge impact on the restaurant menus of today, but back in the early 1980s butchers did not know how to get rid of them; now they are so much in demand that premium prices are obtained for what should be classed as a cheap cut. The lamb shank, affectionately called "souris" (mouse) in French, has often featured on Le Gavroche menus over the years and this recipe always pleases me.

Using a boning knife, trim the lamb shanks at the thin end to reveal the bone. Scrape clean so you have about 1½in of bone protruding from a neatly cut piece of meat. Tie with butcher's string to give the shanks a nice even shape.

Place the shanks in a deep pan with the bones pointing up. Add the lamb bones, vegetables, garlic, and bouquet garni, and cover with the chicken stock. Top up with water if necessary to cover by 1in. Add the peppercorns and a generous teaspoon of sea salt, bring to a boil, and skim. Cover with wax paper and turn the heat down very low to barely simmer for 2 hours, or until the meat is tender, but not falling off the bone. Let cool completely in the stock. Gently lift out the shanks, cut off the string, and set aside. Strain the cooking stock and discard the solids.

Madeira sauce

3 shallots, sliced
½ cup butter
2 tablespoons honey
½ bottle (1½ cups) Madeira
1 tablespoon red wine vinegar
7fl oz of the lamb cooking stock

Put the shallots in a thick-bottomed saucepan with half the butter, cook over high heat until well colored. Add the honey and caramelize, but be careful not to burn the honey. Deglaze with the Madeira and vinegar; reduce by half. Add the stock and reduce to a light sauce consistency. Pass through a fine sieve into a clean saucepan, then whisk in the remaining butter to add a glossy finish.

Braised button onions

24 button onions
1 tablespoon olive oil
3 tablespoons butter
¼ cup port
2 cups veal stock (page 264)

Immerse the onions in very hot water for 20 seconds, then peel. Heat the oil and butter in a thick-bottomed wide pan until foaming; add the onions, and roll in the pan until well browned all over. Pour in the port and reduce by half. Add the stock and again reduce by half, until the onions are tender and glistening golden brown.

Gratin dauphinois

1 ¾ lb white potatoes
2½ cups heavy cream
white pepper
salt
freshly grated nutmeg
1 garlic clove, halved

Heat the oven to 275°F. Peel the potatoes and slice thinly into a bowl; do not put them into water as this will remove the starch that holds the gratin together. Pour in the cream, a little pepper, salt, and nutmeg; mix well without breaking the potatoes. Rub an enameled cast-iron gratin dish (2–2½in deep) with the garlic clove dipped in salt, spread the potato mixture evenly in this dish and bake for 1 hour. Let rest for at least 30 minutes before serving.

Creamed spinach purée

2¼ lb fresh spinach leaves, washed
⅓ cup heavy cream
1 garlic clove, finely chopped
salt
nutmeg

Blanch the spinach in salted boiling water for 1 minute; drain, and refresh in ice-cold water. Drain and press dry, using both hands to squeeze out all the moisture. Transfer to a chopping board and chop finely.

Bring the cream to a boil and add the garlic; reduce by half. Add the spinach and reheat in the cream. Season with salt and a little freshly grated nutmeg.

To assemble: Heat the oven to 425°F. Put the lamb shanks in a roasting pan with 2 tablespoons of butter and place in the oven. After 10 minutes, pour in 1¼ cups of Madeira sauce and baste the shanks. Repeat every 5 minutes for 30 minutes. The shanks should have a caramel-like glaze.

Roast woodcock with grapes and marc

Serves 6

6 woodcock

2 chicken livers

2oz duck foie gras

4 shallots, finely chopped

1 sprig of thyme

salt and pepper

1 tablespoon brandy

30 white seedless grapes

1 tablespoon marc (or grappa)

1 tablespoon caster sugar

4 tablespoons olive oil

½ cup butter

6 pieces of brioche bread,

2in square

2 cups game stock (page 265)

sherry vinegar

I find that woodcock need no more than 1 week of hanging; after that the exquisite aroma is lost in the gaminess.

The old-fashioned way to roast a woodcock is with the guts left in. I prefer to remove them and use them for a liver paste. The only part that is not edible is the gizzard, which is often full of sand; find it by pressing with your fingers. Discard the gizzard, eyes, and tongue, which is believed to be bitter.

To the innards add the chicken liver, foie gras, two of the shallots, and the thyme. Heat a frying pan with a drop of oil until smoking. Add the liver mixture and cook for 15 seconds, turning frequently. Season and then flambé with the brandy. Press through a coarse sieve while still hot. Mix well with a whisk to emulsify. Keep in the refrigerator.

Blanch the grapes in boiling water for 10 seconds; refresh in cold water, then peel with a small knife. Marinate in the marc and sugar for at least 1 hour.

Heat the oven to 425°F. Put the birds in a roasting pan with a little oil and place over high heat until evenly colored. Add most of the butter and place in the oven; cook for 3 minutes on each side and 4 minutes on their backs. Let rest on a rack in a warm place for 15 minutes.

Toast the brioche on both sides, then spread the liver paste over them. Reheat in the oven for 5 minutes before serving.

Remove the fat from the roasting pan and add ½ tablespoon of butter with the remaining shallots. Cook for 2 minutes and then pour in the grapes' marinade and reduce by half. Add the stock and reduce to a light sauce consistency. Whisk in 1 tablespoon of butter, and reheat the grapes in the sauce at the last moment. A few drops of sherry vinegar will bring out the sweet and sour freshness of this sauce.

Gigot d'agneau de sept heures

Serves 8

1 leg of lamb (about 6¼–7lb)

7oz pork back fat

½ cup butter

2 tablespoons olive oil

1 onion, carrot, and celery stalk

5 strips smoked bacon

2 bottles full-bodied red wine

½ bottle port

salt and pepper

3 quarts veal stock (page 264)

Marinade

½ bottle full-bodied red wine

2 garlic cloves, crushed

1 small onion, thickly sliced

1 carrot, thickly sliced

1 sprig of thyme

1 sprig of rosemary

2 tablespoons virgin olive oil

2 cloves

1 tablespoon white peppercorns

3 tablespoons brandy

2 tablespoons red wine vinegar

Wine suggestion:
Château Latour 1988 (Pauillac)

Trim the leg of lamb by removing the aitch bone and lightly scoring the skin. Cut 4½in long strips of pork back fat (½in square) and use to bard the leg of lamb lengthwise at least six times. Place in the marinade, cover with plastic wrap, and refrigerate. Turn the meat several times a day so the meat absorbs the flavors. Marinate for at least 1 week.

Drain the lamb, reserving the marinated vegetables and the marinade. Heat the butter and oil in a thick-bottomed braising pan, add the leg of lamb, and cook over medium-high heat until golden brown. Remove the lamb from the pan and if the fat is burned, discard it and use fresh butter to cook all the vegetables (including the marinated vegetables) until golden brown. Add the bacon, then deglaze the pan with the wine, port, and marinade. Place over high heat and reduce by two-thirds, then add the lamb, season well, and cover with the veal stock. Bring to a boil and skim. Check the seasoning. Put a lid on the dish and place in the oven at 275°F for approximately 7 hours! Keep an eye on this as times vary with oven and meat differences. You may have to top up with liquid occasionally. The meat should be tender and nearly falling off the bone.

Take out of the oven and let cool in the sauce. When cold, carefully remove the lamb from the pan and strain the sauce through a fine sieve. Check for seasoning and consistency; reduce the sauce if necessary. Pour the sauce over the meat and keep in the refrigerator overnight.

Reheat gently, basting the meat occasionally. Bring to the table and serve with a spoon; do not attempt to carve. Serve with creamy mashed potatoes.

Loin of venison with sweet peppercorn sauce

Serves 6

1 saddle of venison (about 9lb)
salt and pepper
olive oil
3 tablespoons spiced cranberries
(page 274)

To serve

2 cups mixed wild mushrooms
1 large celeriac, peeled and cut
into long matchsticks
3 tablespoons butter
7fl oz heavy cream

I try to use roe deer when possible but fallow deer is equally good; ask your butcher for it to be well hung (2 weeks).

Bone out the saddle and remove all fat and sinew from the loins; the trimmings can be used for stock. Cut the loins into 12 noisettes, season lightly, then cook over fierce heat in a frying pan with a little oil. Sear on all the sides; by the time the meat is seared it will nearly be cooked pink. Remove from the pan to rest in a warm place and to finish cooking.

Drain the fat from the pan and add 3 tablespoons of the cranberry cooking liquid. When well reduced add 7fl oz of the sauce poivrade, bring to a boil, and whisk in some green peppercorn butter followed by the cranberries.

Garnish with wild mushrooms simply cooked in a little olive oil, and creamed celeriac: Sweat the celeriac with the butter, stirring occasionally. Season with salt and pepper. When softened but still crunchy add the cream and turn up the heat; cook until the cream has almost all evaporated.

Sauce poivrade

6 shallots, sliced
1 tablespoon crushed white and
black peppercorns
2 tablespoons redcurrant jelly
3 tablespoons red wine vinegar
1¼ cups full-bodied red wine
½ cup port
2½ cups game stock (page 265)

Cook the shallots with a little vegetable oil until caramelized. Add the crushed peppercorns and redcurrant jelly and stir until completely melted. Pour in the vinegar, and let it boil away. Pour in the wine and port and reduce by half. Add the stock and reduce by half again. Pass through a fine sieve into a clean saucepan. Season and, over medium heat, whisk in 2 tablespoons of green peppercorn butter.

Green peppercorn butter

Soften ½ cup unsalted butter and mix in 2 tablespoons drained green peppercorns in brine.

Rich braised stuffed hare

Serves 8

*1 hare, skinned, with its heart,
liver, kidneys, and lungs*

2 shallots, finely chopped

a little butter

*2 cups button mushrooms, roughly
chopped*

*3oz smoked belly of pork
(or bacon)*

¾lb fatty pork belly

3oz pork back fat

2 chicken livers

1lb 2oz uncooked foie gras

1 egg

salt, pepper, and nutmeg

a little Cognac

2 sprigs of thyme, chopped

2 sprigs of parsley, chopped

1 sprig of rosemary, chopped

3–4oz truffle, chopped (optional)

9oz caul fat (crépinette), rinsed

It is always worth trying to get rifle-shot hares, rather than cartridge-shot, as the latter are often peppered with little holes and lead. Don't forget to either ask for the blood or collect it yourself, as this is essential to thicken and enrich the sauce. This recipe is not easy and the taste is very gamey: Make sure you invite people who will appreciate your hard work! I find the best way to serve this is to spoon the hare into chunks; do not attempt to slice it as this will just make a mess.

Turn the hare belly up. If it has not been gutted, remove all the guts, keeping the heart, liver (making sure to remove the gall bladder), kidneys, and lungs. Using a boning knife, bone out the whole hare, taking care not to make too many holes. There is no secret or easy way to do this, just slowly follow the bones and think before you cut. When you get to the rib cage, cut through and remove the shoulders. Bone out the shoulders and put the meat from these with the offal.

Sweat the shallots in a knob of butter for 3 minutes, then add the mushrooms and cook until dry; set aside to cool.

Finely mince the hare offal and shoulder meat with all the pork belly and fat, chicken livers, mushroom and shallot mixture, and about 7oz of the foie gras. Add the egg, season well with salt, pepper, nutmeg, and Cognac, and beat well to bind this forcemeat together. Mix in the herbs and the truffle, if using, then take a spoonful of the forcemeat and cook in a frying pan to check the seasoning.

Cut the remaining foie gras in half lengthwise, season well, and sprinkle with a little Cognac; cover and set aside.

Spread two layers of caul fat on a work surface, put the boned hare on top, open it out, and season well. Push some forcemeat into the leg cavities, then spread the forcemeat all

To braise

5 cups full-bodied red wine

1¼ cups port

2 onions, 2 celery stalks, and

1 carrot, roughly chopped

2 tablespoons olive oil

2 tablespoons butter

6 juniper berries, crushed

½ teaspoon cracked black

peppercorns

1 bay leaf

3 tablespoons brandy

2 quarts game stock (page 265) or

veal stock (page 264)

To finish the sauce

⅔ cup butter

the hare blood

over to a thickness of ½in. Place the two strips of foie gras in the center and cover with the rest of the forcemeat, pressing it down well. Roll the hare over itself to envelop the stuffing completely, overlapping where possible to make an even bolster shape, then wrap with the caul fat, tucking it in at each end. Using kitchen string, tie up the hare, firstly lengthwise and then widthwise, approximately 30 times.

To braise, boil the wine and port to reduce by half. In a casserole dish just big enough to take the hare, caramelize the vegetables with the oil and butter. Push the vegetables to the side and add the hare; brown lightly on all sides. Add the juniper, peppercorns, and bay leaf, and flambé with the brandy. Pour in the reduced wine and stock to cover; season lightly. Bring to a boil, skim, and then turn down to a simmer; cover with wax paper. Place in the oven at 250°F for 4 hours. The meat should be very soft and easily pierced with a needle or small knife. Let cool completely in the sauce, and refrigerate overnight.

To serve: Heat the oven to 325°F. Remove the layer of fat from the top of the sauce and discard. Take out the hare, cut off the string, and put the hare into a deep, ovenproof serving dish. Bring the sauce to a boil, skim well, and pass through a fine sieve; pour half over the hare, cover with a lid, and place in the oven to reheat for 35–45 minutes.

Reheat the rest of the sauce and whisk in the butter. Remove from the heat and whisk in the blood; do not boil or it will curdle. Pass through a fine sieve if necessary.

Serve with potatoes mashed with cream and butter, to which you have added some lightly crushed cooked chestnuts.

Whisky gelatin with oranges and Drambuie sauce

Serves 10

6 sheets of gelatin
1 cup light brown sugar
1 tablespoon honey
½ cup water
1½ cups whisky
10 oranges

Soften the gelatin in cold water; squeeze dry. Melt the sugar and honey in the water, bring to a boil, then remove from the heat. Whisk in the gelatin and whisky and let cool.

Segment the oranges—use five blood oranges if you like—and dry with paper towels. Line a terrine (10in x 3in x 3in) or individual molds with a layer of gelatin and let set. Add a layer of orange segments, cover with gelatin, and let set again. Repeat, finishing with a layer of gelatin. Refrigerate overnight. Invert, slice, and serve with Drambuie sauce.

Drambuie sauce

1½ cups milk
1 vanilla bean, split
4 egg yolks
⅓ cup sugar
4 tablespoons Drambuie

Bring the milk and vanilla to a boil, then remove from the heat. Beat the yolks and sugar until thick. Pour the boiling milk on to the yolk mixture, whisking continuously. Return to the saucepan and stir over low heat until the custard thickens slightly. Let cool slightly before adding the Drambuie.

*Soccer star David Ginola and his wife
Coraline wishing us a new century full
of sunshine and love*

Christmas stuffed baked apples

Serves 8

¼lb suet

⅔ cup light brown sugar

1½ cups grated cooking apples

⅔ cup golden raisins

⅓ cup raisins

½ cup dried prunes, chopped

¼ cup walnuts, chopped

¼ cup almonds, chopped

1 teaspoon ground cinnamon

½ teaspoon mixed spice

1 generous shot of dark rum and

1 of brandy

8 Cox's or other tart green apples

⅔ cup butter

confectioner's sugar

1 glass of brandy for the sauce

Mix the suet and muscovado sugar with the grated apples, dried fruit, nuts, spices, rum, and brandy. The flavoring is very much a matter of taste; you may like more cinnamon, for example. This mixture can be kept in the refrigerator in an airtight container for many weeks, and if anything it improves with storage.

Heat the oven to 400°F. Peel the Cox's apples and remove the cores. Fill each apple with the stuffing, packing it tightly; there will be plenty, so pile the stuffing up to cover the top of the apple. Put the apples in a roasting pan and put a knob of butter on each apple. Liberally sprinkle with confectioner's sugar and place in the oven for 20 minutes, basting often with the cooking juices.

Serve the apples on warmed plates. Place the roasting pan over high heat and pour in a good glass of brandy, whisking to loosen all the caramelized juices in the tray. Pass through a sieve into a pitcher and pour over the apples.

Serve hot, with chilled crème fraîche or muscovado sugar ice cream.

Muscovado sugar ice cream

3 cups milk

1 cup light cream

12 egg yolks

1¼ cups dark muscovado sugar

Bring the milk and cream to a boil, then remove from the heat. Beat the yolks and sugar until thick and creamy. Pour the boiling milk into the yolk mixture, whisking continuously. Return the mixture to the saucepan and stir with a wooden spatula over low heat until the custard thickens slightly. Chill, then churn in an ice-cream machine until frozen.

Wine suggestion:

Saussignac, Château Tourmentine
1994, J M Hure

Turkish orange salad with pistachio ice cream

Serves 10

10 oranges and 10 blood oranges
2¾ cups water
2¼ cups sugar
5 cloves, plus extra, to serve
2 tablespoons clarified butter
2 tablespoons clear honey
4 sheets of pastilla/brique (North African paper-thin pancakes, similar to filo pastry)

Pare off the zest of four of the oranges. Make a clove syrup by boiling the water with the sugar, cloves, and orange zest for 1 minute; cover and let cool.

Peel another four oranges with a vegetable peeler, taking care not to remove any of the white pith. Cut the zest into thin julienne strips. Place in a small saucepan, cover with cold water, and bring to a boil, then drain and repeat the process twice. Finish by simmering the zest in a little of the clove syrup for 10 minutes. Let cool

Heat the oven to 325°F. Gently heat the butter and honey together. Delicately brush the sheets of brique with the butter and honey, then place on a baking sheet and bake until crisp, 6–7 minutes. Let cool.

To serve: Peel and segment all the oranges and arrange in soup plates. Sprinkle with the confit of zest and strain the syrup over the top. Scoop the ice cream into the center of the plates. Break the pastry into shards and stick into the ice cream. Put some cloves in a pepper mill and give a few turns on top of the oranges.

Pistachio ice cream

6 egg yolks
½ cup caster sugar
2 cups whole milk
¼ cup pistachio paste
¼ cup peeled pistachios, roughly chopped

Whisk the egg yolks with half the sugar in a large bowl until thick and creamy. Bring the milk and remaining sugar to a boil. Remove from the heat, add the pistachio paste, and stir to dissolve. Pour the hot milk into the yolk mixture and stir well. Return the mixture to the saucepan and stir over low heat until the mixture thickens enough to coat the spatula. Chill, then strain the mixture into an ice-cream machine, and churn until frozen but not too stiff. Stir in the pistachios and freeze until required.

Rum baba with cream and poached pineapple

12 babas

½ cake compressed yeast

1 ½ tablespoons warm milk

2 teaspoons salt

4½ cups bread flour

5 eggs

1 tablespoon sugar

⅔ cup unsalted butter, softened
and cut into small pieces

⅓ cup dark rum

Put the yeast and milk in the bowl of an electric mixer bowl and stir until dissolved. Using the dough hook attachment, mix in the salt, flour, eggs, and sugar, and knead for 10 minutes until the dough is smooth and elastic. Cover with a damp cloth and let rise in a warm place for 1 hour.

Still using the dough hook, beat in the softened butter, a little at a time. When completely incorporated, the dough should be smooth and glossy. Use the dough to three-quarters fill your 12 molds: Either classic baba molds (2½in x 2in), preferably non-stick, or round savarin molds, 2¾in in diameter. Let rise for 15–20 minutes.

Heat the oven to 375°F. Cook the babas for about 20 minutes, until they are a rich brown color.

Tip the babas out of the molds on to a wire rack to cool. Prick the babas with a needle to help them soak up the syrup. Put them in the warmed soaking syrup, turning them over after 10 minutes to make sure they are evenly soaked. Using a perforated spoon, carefully remove the babas from the syrup, and put on a rack to drain the excess syrup.

Soaking syrup

1 quart water

2⅔ cups caster sugar

1 cinnamon stick

2 strips of pared orange rind

Put all the ingredients into a large saucepan, bring to a boil, and then strain.

Poached pineapple

1 pineapple

3 cups water

2 cups caster sugar

Peel the pineapple and cut into round slices, ½in thick. Bring the sugar and water to a boil and then add the pineapple; turn down the heat and simmer for 8 minutes. Let cool in the syrup.

When cold, drain and cut each slice into four wedges. Reserve 24 evenly shaped wedges. Blend the remaining pineapple with a little of the poaching syrup to make a sauce.

Pineapple crisps

Heat the oven to 275°F. Peel a small pineapple and slice as thinly as possible. Place in a single layer on a non-stick baking sheet and sprinkle lightly with confectioner's sugar. Place in the oven for 20 minutes or until the pineapple has completely dried out. While still warm, place on a cold, dry, flat surface. As soon as the pineapple crisps are completely cold and set, place in an airtight container to keep crisp.

Chantilly cream

1 ½ cups whipping cream

⅓ cup confectioner's sugar

2 teaspoons vanilla extract

(optional)

Whisk the cream together with the sugar and vanilla until it forms soft peaks.

To serve: Gently pour a generous shot of dark rum over each baba. Serve with a spoonful of Chantilly cream, two wedges of poached pineapple, and a pineapple crisp, and drizzle the pineapple sauce around the plate.

Drink suggestion:

Vieux Rhum, Bailly 1966 'Martinique'

Banana soufflé with rum and caramel sauce

Serves 8

3 over-ripe bananas
4 tablespoons water
juice of 1 lemon
3 tablespoons caster sugar
1 tablespoon cornflour
2 tablespoons dark rum

Peel and slice the bananas and put in a saucepan over medium heat with the water, lemon juice, and sugar. Simmer for 5 minutes, squashing with the back of a fork . Transfer to a blender and blend until smooth. Return to the pan and, over high heat, whisk in the cornflour that has been dissolved in the rum. Bring to a boil, then remove from the heat. Cover with plastic wrap to prevent a crust from forming.

Glazed and fried bananas

5 bananas
confectioner's sugar
3 tablespoons unsalted butter
3 tablespoons demerara sugar
3 tablespoons dark rum

Slice one banana into eight, dust with confectioner's sugar, and caramelize with a blowtorch or under a hot broiler; repeat twice to get a good layer of glaze.

Cut the other four bananas into large dice and fry in the butter over high heat. After 30 seconds add the demerara sugar and toss in the pan for 2 minutes, until caramelized. Add the rum and cook for 15 seconds. Remove from the heat and keep warm.

Caramel sauce

¼ cup caster sugar
3 tablespoons water
1½ cups heavy cream

In a thick-bottomed saucepan, bring the sugar and water to a boil. Brush down the inside of the pan with a pastry brush dipped in cold water to prevent crystals from forming. Continue cooking until the sugar turns an amber-brown caramel color. Turn off the heat and slowly whisk in the cream, then pass through a fine sieve.

256

8 egg whites

⅓ cup caster sugar, plus extra for
the soufflé molds

To assemble: Heat the oven to 375°F. Butter eight ramekins (3½in diameter x 2½in deep). Coat the insides of the ramekins with sugar, tipping out any excess.

Whisk the egg whites until frothy. Add the sugar and continue whisking until firm. Mix one-third of the egg whites with the banana purée until smooth, then lightly fold in the rest of the egg whites.

Half fill the ramekins with the mixture. Put a spoonful of the fried bananas into each and cover with the rest of the mixture. Smooth the surface with a palette knife, then run the tip of a knife around the inside of the ramekins to help the soufflés to rise evenly.

Place in the oven and cook for 7–8 minutes. The soufflés should remain moist in the middle. Serve immediately, dusted with confectioner's sugar. Place a slice of glazed banana on top. Serve the caramel sauce separately, to be poured into the soufflé at table by making a little hole in the top.

Hot chocolate soufflé

Serves 8

1 ¾ cups milk

1 vanilla bean

⅓ cup unsalted butter, softened

½ cup all-purpose flour

3 tablespoons unsweetened cocoa powder

6 eggs, separated, plus 6 extra whites

3oz unsweetened chocolate (64–70% cocoa solids), chopped

1 tablespoon rum or liqueur, such as Grand Marnier

3 tablespoons caster sugar

For really stiff, smooth egg whites, freeze them up to a week ahead and defrost on the day you want to use them.

Bring the milk to a boil with the vanilla. Beat the butter until smooth, sift in the flour and cocoa powder, pour in the hot milk, then return to the pan and bring back to a boil over high heat, whisking continuously. Remove from the heat and whisk in the egg yolks, chopped chocolate, and rum or liqueur. Cover with buttered wax paper and set aside.

Heat the oven to 375°F. Butter 8 ramekins (3½in diameter x 2½in deep) and sprinkle with a little cocoa powder, tipping out any excess.

Whisk the chocolate mixture until smooth. Whisk all the egg whites in an electric mixer until frothy, then add the sugar, 1 tablespoon at a time, and continue whisking until stiff yet still smooth. Beat one-third of the egg whites into the chocolate mixture until smooth, then gently fold in the rest.

If you like, place a couple of rum-soaked macaroons (page 52) in each ramekin before you add the soufflé mixture.

Pour the soufflé mixture into the ramekins, smooth the surface with a palette knife, and then run the point of a knife around the rim: This helps them to rise evenly. Place in the oven for 11 minutes; the soufflés should still be creamy in the middle. Serve immediately, dusted with a little confectioner's sugar, along with a sauceboat of hot rich chocolate sauce.

Wine suggestion:
Madeira, Malmsey 1863, Leacocks

Rich chocolate sauce

1 cup light cream

1 ½ tablespoons caster sugar

4oz unsweetened chocolate, chopped

2 tablespoons butter

Boil the cream with the sugar. Remove from the heat and beat in the chocolate and butter; keep warm but do not boil. This can be refrigerated and gently reheated in a double boiler.

Warm bitter chocolate tart with ivory ice cream

Serves 8

sweet pastry dough (page 279)
3 eggs
4 egg yolks
¾ cup caster sugar
13oz unsweetened bitter chocolate
(70% cocoa solids)
1 cup plus 2 tablespoons unsalted
butter

Roll out the pastry dough and use to line a flan ring (10in diameter x ¾in deep). Cover the bottom of the tart shell with a circle of wax paper and some dried beans and bake blind for 20 minutes at 350°F. Take out the beans and paper and return to the oven for 5 minutes to cook the tart shell completely. Turn the oven down to 275°F.

Whisk the eggs, yolks, and sugar in an electric mixer at full speed until pale and frothy, about 5 minutes. Melt the chopped chocolate and butter in a double boiler, then fold into the egg mixture. Pour into the shell bottom and immediately place in the oven for 15 minutes. Remove from the oven and let cool to tepid.

Ivory ice cream

2 cups milk
6 egg yolks
½ cup caster sugar
12oz white chocolate, chopped

Bring the milk to a boil. Beat the egg yolks with the sugar until thick and creamy. Pour on the hot milk, whisking continuously. Return the mixture to the saucepan and cook over low heat, stirring continuously with a rubber spatula, until the custard thickens slightly. While still warm, stir in the white chocolate. Let cool, then churn in an ice-cream machine until frozen.

To serve: Cut the chocolate tart into slices and serve with a scoop of ivory ice cream in a chocolate brandy snap. Drizzle a little bitter orange sauce around the plate.

Wine suggestion:
Rasteau 1995, Domaine la Soumade

Bitter orange sauce

7fl oz fresh orange juice
1½ cup caster sugar
2 tablespoons bitter orange marmalade

Boil the orange juice and sugar until reduced by three-quarters. Add the marmalade, stir to melt, and then pass through a fine sieve. Let cool.

Chocolate brandy snap

¼ cup butter, softened
¼ cup light corn syrup
½ cup all-purpose flour
3 tablespoons unsweetened cocoa powder
⅔ cup caster sugar

Beat the butter with the sugar and light corn syrup, then fold in the flour and cocoa powder. Let rest in the refrigerator for 24 hours.

Heat the oven to 350°F. Spread the mixture thinly on a non-stick baking sheet, flattening it with moistened fingers. Cook for 8 minutes. Let cool on the baking sheet for a few seconds, then cut out circles and, using a palette knife to lift them off the baking sheet, place them in a tea cup or small rounded mold to set. These can be stored in an airtight container for several days.

The singer and former Goon Harry Secombe sings in praise of Le Gavroche

Stocks, Sau

ces, Pastries

White chicken stock

Makes about 4 quarts

4½lb chicken bones or wing tips
1 calf's foot, split
5 quarts water
1 onion
1 small leek
2 celery stalks
2 sprigs of thyme
6 parsley stalks

Place the bones and calf's foot in a large saucepan, cover with the water, and bring to a boil. Skim off the scum and fat that come to the surface. Turn the heat down, add the remaining ingredients, and simmer for 1½ hours, skimming occasionally.

Pass through a fine sieve and let cool. This can be kept in the refrigerator for up to 5 days, or frozen.

Veal stock

Makes about 3½ quarts

3–3½lb veal knuckle bones, chopped
1 calf's foot, split
1 large onion, roughly chopped
2 large carrots, roughly chopped
1 celery stalk, roughly chopped
5 quarts water
2 garlic cloves
2 sprigs of thyme
½ tablespoon tomato paste

Roast the bones and calf's foot in a hot oven (425°F), turning occasionally until brown all over, then put them into a large saucepan.

Put the onion, carrots, and celery into the roasting pan and roast until golden, turning frequently with a wooden spatula. Pour off any excess fat and put the roasted vegetables into the saucepan with the bones.

Put the roasting pan over high heat and add 2 cups of the water to deglaze the pan; scrape the bottom with a wooden spatula to loosen all the caramelized sugars, then pour into the saucepan with the bones.

Add the remaining ingredients and bring to a boil. Skim off the scum and fat that come to the surface. Turn down the heat and simmer gently for 3½ hours, skimming occasionally.

Pass through a fine sieve and let cool. This can be kept in the refrigerator for 8–10 days, or frozen.

Beef stock for soup or consommé

Makes about 5 quarts

6½–7lb beef bones, chopped
3 pig's feet, split
2 onions, roughly chopped
1 carrot, roughly chopped
2 celery stalks, roughly chopped
2 bay leaves
1 sprig of thyme
1 bunch of parsley stalks
2 teaspoons white and black
peppercorns
3 beefsteak tomatoes, chopped
1 leek top (green part)

Roast the bones and pig's feet in a hot oven (425°F), turning occasionally until brown all over, then put them into a deep saucepan. Add water to cover by 6in.

Pour off some of the fat from the roasting pan, add the onions, carrot, and celery, and roast until golden, turning frequently with a wooden spatula. Add the roasted vegetables and all the other ingredients to the bones.

Put the roasting pan over high heat and add 2 cups of water to deglaze the pan; scrape the bottom with a wooden spatula to loosen all the caramelized sugars, then pour into the saucepan with the bones.

Bring to a boil, skim off the scum and fat that come to the surface, then lower the heat and simmer for 2½ hours, skimming frequently. Strain and chill. This can be kept in the refrigerator for up to 7 days, or frozen.

Game stock

Makes about 3½ quarts

4½lb game bones (rabbit,
mallard, venison—alternatively,
buy a wild rabbit and an old cock
pheasant)
1 calf's foot, split
1 onion, roughly chopped
1 carrot, roughly chopped
2 celery stalks, roughly chopped
6 juniper berries, crushed

Roast the bones and calf's foot in a hot oven (425°F) with a little oil until well browned. Place in a deep saucepan and cover with water.

Put the onion, carrot, and celery into the roasting pan and roast until brown, then add to the saucepan with the bones.

Put the roasting pan over high heat and add 1 quart of cold water; scrape the bottom with a wooden spatula to loosen the caramelized sugars. Bring to a boil, then pour into the saucepan with the bones; add the juniper berries.

Simmer for 2 hours, occasionally skimming off the fat and scum that come to the surface. Pass through a sieve and chill. This can be kept in the refrigerator for up to 7 days, or frozen.

Court bouillon

Makes about 2¼ quarts

2 carrots

white part of 1 leek

1 celery stalk

½ fennel bulb

4 shallots

2 small white onions

1½ quarts water

1 bottle dry white wine

2 tablespoons white wine vinegar

1 bouquet garni

1½ tablespoons coarse sea salt

1 tablespoon cracked black or
white peppercorns

Peel the carrots, leek, celery, fennel, shallots, and onions, then slice into thin (⅛in) circles.

Put the water, wine, and vinegar in a saucepan, and bring to a boil, then add all the vegetables, bouquet garni, salt, and the peppercorns tied in a little cheesecloth bag. Simmer for 15 minutes, until the vegetables are cooked but still a little crunchy. Strain and chill.

This can be kept in the refrigerator for 3–4 days. The vegetables can be used as part of a recipe.

Fish stock

Makes about 2 quarts

2¼lb bones and heads from white
fish (e.g., sole, whiting, turbot)

1 small onion, roughly chopped

1 celery stalk, roughly chopped

4 tablespoons butter

½ cup dry white wine

2 quarts water

6 parsley stalks

1 bay leaf

Remove any gills from the fish heads; soak the heads and bones in cold water for 3–4 hours.

Roughly chop the fish bones and heads. Sweat the onion and celery with the butter in a deep saucepan over low heat. When softened, add the fish bones and heads, and cook for 2–3 minutes, stirring frequently. Pour in the wine, turn up the heat, and reduce by half. Add the water and herbs and bring to a boil, skimming frequently. Lower the heat and simmer, uncovered, for 25 minutes.

Strain through a cheesecloth-lined sieve and let cool. This can be kept in the refrigerator for 2–3 days, or frozen.

Lobster stock

Makes about 3 quarts

6½–7lb lobster heads
1 large onion, chopped
1 carrot, chopped
2 celery stalks, chopped
2 tablespoons olive oil
4 sprigs of parsley stalks
1 sprig of thyme
1 bay leaf
2 large tomatoes
2 tablespoons tomato paste
½ teaspoon cayenne pepper, plus extra, to serve
1 tablespoon brandy
1¼ cups dry white wine
2 quarts fish stock
1 quart veal stock
sea salt

I have specified lobster heads, because the claw and body bones have little flavor (although by all means add them if you have room in the pan). Norwegian lobster (langoustine) and shrimp heads can also be added.

Crush the lobster heads with a mallet or a rolling pin until they are well broken up. Sweat the onion, carrot, and celery with the olive oil in a large saucepan. When the vegetables are lightly browned, add the herbs and lobster heads, stirring to prevent sticking. After about 5 minutes, when the bones are hot, stir in the tomatoes, tomato paste, and cayenne pepper. Pour in the brandy and stir well for a minute or two, then add the wine, and boil for at least 3 minutes.

Add the stocks and bring to a boil; season lightly with sea salt. Simmer for 40 minutes, stirring occasionally, and skimming off the scum that appears on the surface.

Drain through a colander set over a large bowl, pressing the lobster heads well to extract all the juices and flavor. Then pass this liquid through a fine sieve into a clean saucepan. Bring to a boil and skim. This can be kept in the refrigerator for 2–3 days, or frozen.

Bouquet garni

2 sprigs of thyme
6 parsley stalks
½ celery stalk
2 bay leaves

This is the basic bouquet garni; it can be varied by including other herbs, such as basil stalks.

Place the ingredients in a bundle and tie together with string.

Chicken jus

Makes about 2 quarts

*2¼lb chicken bones, chopped
small*
3 shallots, chopped
½ cup dry white wine
2½ quarts white chicken stock

Roast the bones in a hot oven (425°F), turning occasionally until browned, then place in a deep saucepan.

Brown the shallots in the roasting pan, stirring frequently. Add the wine and stir with a wooden spatula to loosen the caramelized residue. Boil to reduce by half, then pour into the saucepan with the bones. Add the stock and bring to a boil. Simmer for 45 minutes, skimming occasionally, then strain.

Duck jus

Makes about 2½ quarts

4½lb duck bones
1 onion, sliced
3 shallots, sliced
1 cup port
3 quarts white chicken stock

Chop the bones and remove any excess fat. Roast in a hot oven (425°F) until browned, then drain off excess fat and put the bones in a deep saucepan.

Brown the onion and shallots in the roasting pan, stirring frequently. Pour in the port and stir with a rubber spatula to loosen the caramelized residue. Boil to reduce by half, then pour over the bones. Add the stock and bring to a boil. Simmer for 45 minutes, then strain.

Lamb jus

Makes about 2 quarts

3lb lamb bones, chopped small
1 onion, sliced
2 sprigs of thyme
2 garlic cloves
1 cup dry white wine
2½ quarts veal stock

Roast the bones in a hot oven (425°F), turning occasionally until browned, then place in a deep saucepan.

Brown the onion in the roasting pan, stirring frequently. Add the wine and stir with a wooden spatula to loosen the caramelized residue. Boil to reduce by half, then pour into the saucepan with the bones. Add the thyme, garlic, and stock, and bring to a boil. Simmer for 45 minutes, skimming occasionally, then strain.

Red wine sauce

Makes about 1½ quarts

¼lb beef trimmings (bone or sinew), optional
a little olive oil
1 bottle full-bodied red wine (e.g., Syrah / Shiraz)
½ cup port
1 onion, sliced
2 shallots, sliced
3 strips smoked bacon, chopped
1 teaspoon cracked white and black peppercorns
2 quarts veal stock

If you have some beef trimmings, fry them in a saucepan with a little oil until crisp. Drain off the fat and add the wine and port; reduce by half, occasionally skimming off the fat and scum that come to the surface.

In another saucepan, cook the onion, shallots, and bacon with a little oil until well browned. Add the pepper and then pour in the reduced wine, followed by the veal stock. Bring to a boil and skim, then turn down the heat and simmer for 35 minutes. Pass through a fine sieve. This can be kept in the refrigerator for up to 7 days, or frozen.

To serve with steaks, bring the sauce to a boil and reduce until slightly thickened. Remove from the heat and whisk in a little cold butter, cut into small pieces.

Tarragon sauce

Makes about 1 cup

2 shallots, finely chopped
2 tablespoons unsalted butter
2 tablespoons tarragon vinegar
½ cup dry white wine
1¾ cups white chicken stock
½ cup heavy cream
salt and freshly ground white pepper
5 tablespoons tarragon leaves

This delicate sauce can accompany chicken or poached fish. Do not strain it, as the texture of the shallots adds another dimension to the sauce.

Sweat the shallots with half the butter in a saucepan over low heat. When the shallots are soft, but have not begun to color, deglaze the pan with the tarragon vinegar and white wine; reduce this liquid until nearly dry.

Pour in the chicken stock and reduce until syrupy. Add the cream and boil for 2 minutes, then whisk in the remaining butter, season to taste and, just before serving, add the freshly chopped tarragon.

Hollandaise sauce

Makes about ⅔ cup

1 cup unsalted butter
2 teaspoons white wine vinegar
1 teaspoon cracked white
peppercorns
pinch of salt
4 egg yolks
lemon juice

Melt the butter in a small saucepan over low heat until it foams, spoon off the foam, and let the butter settle. Remove the clarified butter with a ladle, discarding the whitish residue in the bottom of the pan.

Boil the vinegar with the pepper and salt, then remove from the heat, add 2 tablespoons of water and the egg yolks, transfer to a double boiler (not too hot) and whisk until the egg yolks are light and creamy, 8–10 minutes. Do not let the mixture get too hot, otherwise the eggs will scramble.

Remove from the heat and, whisking continuously, gently pour in the clarified butter. Pass through a fine sieve, and add a little lemon juice to taste.

Beurre blanc

Makes about 1¼ cups

½ cup dry white wine
1 tablespoon white wine vinegar
2 shallots, finely chopped
3 tablespoons heavy cream
¾ cup cold unsalted butter, cubed
salt and pepper

Put the wine, vinegar, and shallots in a thick-bottomed saucepan, bring to a boil, and reduce by half. Then add the cream and boil for 1 minute. Lower the heat and gradually whisk in the cubes of cold butter.

I like to keep the shallots in the sauce, but if you prefer a smooth finish, pass the sauce through a fine sieve. Season with salt and pepper to taste.

Béarnaise sauce

Makes about ¼ cup

1 cup plus 2 tablespoons unsalted butter

2 shallots, finely chopped

3 tablespoons snipped fresh tarragon

3 tablespoons white wine vinegar or tarragon vinegar

1 teaspoon crushed white peppercorns

4 egg yolks

2 tablespoons snipped fresh chervil

In a small saucepan, melt the butter over low heat until it foams, spoon off the foam and let the butter settle. Remove the clarified butter with a ladle, discarding the whitish residue in the bottom of the pan.

Put the shallots in a shallow pan with the tarragon, vinegar, pepper, and 1 tablespoon of water; boil to reduce by half. Remove from the heat and let cool.

When cold, add the egg yolks and whisk in a double boiler (not too hot) until the yolks are light and creamy, 8–10 minutes. Do not let the mixture get too hot, otherwise the eggs will scramble.

Remove from the heat and, whisking continuously, gently pour in the clarified butter. Season to taste and add the chervil just before serving

Sauce paloise

Use fresh mint instead of tarragon and chervil. Delicious with broiled lamb.

Sauce choron

Peel, deseed, and chop 5 ripe plum tomatoes and sweat in a little butter to remove excess moisture. Add to the finished Béarnaise sauce.

271

Herb vinaigrette

Makes about 2 cups

2 egg yolks
1 teaspoon Dijon mustard
1 ½ tablespoons tarragon vinegar
salt and freshly ground white
pepper
⅔ cup extra virgin olive oil
1 ¼ cups vegetable oil
1 tablespoon each of chives, flat-leaf parsley and tarragon, chopped

Put the yolks in a blender with the mustard, vinegar, salt, and pepper, and blend at high speed, slowly adding the oil, a little at a time. After one-third of the oil has been incorporated, add the herbs. Continue to blend, adding the oil a little at a time. The vinaigrette should have the consistency of pouring cream; if the mixture becomes too thick, add a few drops of cold water to the blender.

If you want to remove the herbs, pass the vinaigrette through a fine sieve. This can be kept in the refrigerator for up to 2 weeks.

Tomato vinaigrette

Replace the herbs with 1 heaping teaspoon tomato paste and 1 heaping tablespoon of tomato "fondue": 4 ripe tomatoes, peeled, deseeded, and chopped, then cooked gently in a little olive oil until the mixture is thick and dry.

Instead of the pepper in the herb vinaigrette, you could use a few drops of Tabasco sauce.

Mayonnaise

Makes about 2½ cups

2 egg yolks
1 tablespoon Dijon mustard
1 teaspoon fine salt
½ tablespoon white wine vinegar
2 cups vegetable oil
3 tablespoons extra virgin olive oil

Put the yolks, mustard, salt, and vinegar in a round-bottomed bowl and mix with a balloon whisk until smooth. Gradually pour in the oil in a thin steady stream, whisking continuously until rich and creamy.

This can be kept in a covered container in the refrigerator for up to 1 week.

272

Pesto

Makes about 1 cup

7oz basil leaves
¼ cup pine nuts
3 walnuts, roughly chopped
pinch of salt
⅓ cup Parmesan cheese, grated
5–7fl oz extra virgin olive oil

This intensely basil-flavored pesto can be made in a mortar and pestle, and if you are making just a small amount and have plenty of time to spare, go for it. Otherwise, double or treble the quantities given here and make a big batch in a blender; no one will be the wiser.

Put the basil, nuts, and salt in a large mortar and grind with a pestle to form a coarse paste. Work the Parmesan into the paste, then gradually beat in the olive oil with a wooden spoon until you have a thick sauce.

Alternatively, place all ingredients (begin with the smaller amount of oil) except the cheese in a blender and purée briefly at high speed. Add the cheese and blend for a few seconds. The secret of making pesto in a blender is not to overmix it; if the basil is blended for too long it will become hot and lose its bright green color.

If you want the pesto for pasta, broiled fish, or to garnish soup, then keep it fairly coarse and dry. If it is for mixing into a sauce or to use as salad dressing with a little balsamic vinegar, use more oil and blend until smooth.

If stored in a clean airtight jar with a film of oil on top of the pesto, it can be kept in the refrigerator for up to 2 weeks.

Dried tomatoes

Blanch ripe red plum tomatoes in boiling water for 15 seconds, then peel, cut in half lengthwise, and scoop out the seeds. Toss the tomato halves in a little salt, pepper, olive oil, chopped garlic, and thyme leaves. Arrange on a wire rack and place in a very low oven (225°F) for 6 hours or until dry.

Cranberries in spiced port

1 orange
½ lemon
½ cup caster sugar
2 cloves
1 cinnamon stick
1 ¼ cups port
½ cup red wine
4 cups cranberries

These can be added to sauce poivrade (page 245) to be served with game, or to redcurrant jelly to accompany roast turkey or cold chicken. In late September and October it is sometimes possible to buy wild cranberries from the Auvergne region of France; they are tiny but full of flavor. Their larger cousins from America can be used in this recipe and work well even if frozen.

Using a vegetable peeler, peel the rind of the orange and lemon without removing any of the white pith; squeeze the juice of both. Cut half the orange rind and one-third of the lemon rind into thin julienne strips and place in a saucepan with all the juice. Add the sugar, cloves, cinnamon, port, and wine, bring to a boil, and simmer for 2 minutes. Add the cranberries, quickly bring back to a boil, and immediately take off the heat.

Pour into clean glass parfait jars and seal. The cranberries can be kept in the refrigerator for 6 months.

Garlic butter

8–10 garlic cloves, peeled
1 shallot, peeled
1 cup unsalted butter, softened
1 bunch of parsley, washed and
finely chopped
dash of Pernod
salt and freshly ground white
pepper

Slice the garlic in half and remove the green shoots from the center (you will not find this in every garlic clove, but it is especially likely in the winter). Finely chop the garlic and shallot. Place the softened butter in a mixing bowl with the garlic, shallot, and parsley and beat with a wooden spoon, slowly incorporating the Pernod. Season to taste. This can be wrapped in wax paper and frozen.

Wild garlic

Wild garlic can be found in many parts of England and Wales along streams or in valleys where subterranean water runs. The Romans must have been more than happy when they stumbled upon this pungent, garlicky herb. Usually found in great clusters, the strong-scented wide leaf appears in early spring and by May it bears small white edible flowers. The flowers are wonderful in a mixed leaf salad or as fritters, deep-fried in a light batter, for an apéritif.

Wild garlic butter

1 cup unsalted butter, at room temperature
1 tablespoon chopped parsley
1 shallot, chopped
3oz wild garlic leaves, cut into fine julienne
pinch of salt
freshly ground white pepper

Use this to cook fresh shrimp, or as a topping for broiled steaks.

Soften the butter in a small bowl, then beat in all the other ingredients with a wooden spoon. Roll into a log shape and wrap in plastic wrap. This can be kept in the refrigerator for 8–10 days, or frozen.

Mint and wild garlic sauce

1½ oz wild garlic leaves
1 tablespoon fresh mint
½ cup white wine vinegar
4 tablespoons olive oil
2–2½ tablespoons caster sugar
salt and pepper

Serve as a dressing for crisp lettuce salad, or for cold fresh shrimp or lobster.

Shred the wild garlic and mint leaves. Whisk the remaining ingredients together in a small bowl, then stir in the leaves.

Peach chutney

Makes about 4lb

½lb tomatoes

1½ cups light muscovado sugar

¼lb grated peeled apples

grated zest and juice of 2 limes

¼lb onion, chopped

1 garlic clove, chopped

1¼ cups white wine vinegar

1 tablespoon salt

1 tablespoon ground cinnamon

1½ teaspoons ground nutmeg

1½ teaspoons ground white pepper

2 tablespoons ground ginger

2lb peaches

1 cup slivered almonds

This is delicious with boiled ham. It should be left to mature for at least a week before use.

Blanch the tomatoes in boiling water for 15 seconds, then refresh in ice-cold water. Peel, cut in half, and deseed; chop the flesh. Put the tomato flesh into a large, thick-bottomed, non-aluminum saucepan. Add all the remaining ingredients, except the peaches and almonds. Simmer, stirring frequently, until thick and syrupy, about 30 minutes.

Meanwhile, blanch the peaches in boiling water for 10–15 seconds, then refresh in ice-cold water. Peel and cut into large chunks. Add the peaches and almonds to the saucepan and simmer until the peaches are tender, but still holding their shape. Pour into sterilized glass jars and seal while hot. Store in a cool, dark place or refrigerator for up to 6 months.

Spicy prune chutney

Makes about 7lb

2¼lb cooking apples

¾lb onions, chopped

⅓ cup cider vinegar

4½ cups soft brown sugar

1 teaspoon salt

1 teaspoon ground cinnamon

½ teaspoon cayenne pepper

2 teaspoons dry English mustard

1lb tomatoes

1½ cups prunes, cut in half

2 cups golden raisins

Peel, core, and coarsely grate the apples and place in a large, thick-bottomed, non-aluminum saucepan. Add the onions, vinegar, sugar, salt, and spices. Bring to a boil, stirring occasionally, and reduce until the mixture is thick and most of the liquid has evaporated.

Blanch the tomatoes in boiling water for 15 seconds, then refresh in ice-cold water. Peel the tomatoes, cut in half, and remove the seeds, and chop the tomato flesh. Add the tomatoes, prunes, and golden raisins to the saucepan and simmer for about 20 minutes, stirring occasionally, until thick. Pour into sterilized glass jars and seal while hot. Store in a cool, dark place or refrigerator for up to 6 months.

Pear chutney

Makes about 3¹/₂lb

2½ cups caster sugar

¼lb grated peeled cooking apples

¼lb onion, chopped

1 tablespoon coarsely grated
orange rind

juice of 2 oranges

½ tablespoon salt

2oz fresh ginger, chopped

½ teaspoon ground cinnamon

1 teaspoon ground nutmeg

1 teaspoon cayenne pepper

2 pinches of saffron strands

1¼ cups white wine vinegar

1½lb pears

½lb tomatoes

¼ cup golden raisins

This is especially good as an accompaniment to duck dishes, such as duck pot-au-feu (page 238)

Put the sugar in a large, thick-bottomed, non-aluminum saucepan and add the apples, onion, orange rind, and juice, and the salt, spices, and vinegar. Simmer, stirring frequently, until thick and syrupy, about 30 minutes.

Meanwhile, peel, core, and roughly chop the pears. Blanch the tomatoes in boiling water for 15 seconds, then refresh in ice-cold water. Peel the tomatoes, cut in half, and remove the seeds, and chop the tomato flesh. Add the pears, tomatoes, and golden raisins to the saucepan and simmer until the pears are tender. Pour into sterilized glass jars and seal while hot. Store in a cool, dark place, or refrigerator for up to 6 months.

Puff pastry

2 cups unsalted butter

4½ cups all-purpose flour

1 teaspoon salt

1 cup water

Melt 3 tablespoons of the butter and set aside. Sift the flour on to a work surface and make a well in the center. Pour in the melted butter and water with the salt, a little at a time, gradually working the flour into the liquid with your fingertips. When all the flour has been mixed in, lightly knead the dough until it is smooth—it should not be elastic like a bread dough. Form it into a ball and cut a deep cross on the top, cover with plastic wrap, and refrigerate for 2 hours.

Beat the remaining butter with a rolling pin until it becomes pliable, then shape it into a square. Place the dough on a floured work surface and roll out the four corners, leaving a bump in the center. Place the butter on this bump and fold over the four corners, pinching them together to envelop the butter completely.

Roll out to form a rectangle approximately 20in x 8in, then fold the short ends in to the center as if you were folding a letter, to make three equal layers; this is the first turn. Turn this rectangle through 90 degrees and roll out and fold into three as before. Wrap in plastic wrap and refrigerate for 1 hour.

Repeat the rolling and folding three times to give your puff pastry six turns in total.

Quick puff pastry

4½ cups all-purpose flour
2½ cups unsalted butter
1 teaspoon salt
1 cup ice-cold water

This puff pastry is not as delicate as the real thing and will not rise as much; it is, however, a very good substitute.

Sift the flour on to a work surface. Cut the butter into small cubes and add to the flour, with the salt. Using your fingertips, gently mix in the water until all the flour has been incorporated. This dough must not be overworked and some specks of butter should still be visible.

Roll out the dough, fold, and give it two turns, as for puff pastry. Wrap in plastic wrap and refrigerate for 1 hour. Give another two turns, and it is now ready to use.

Sweet pastry dough

1 cup plus 2 tablespoons butter
4½ cups all-purpose flour
pinch of salt
1 cup confectioner's sugar, sifted
4 egg yolks
3 tablespoons water

Cut the butter into small pieces and let soften at room temperature. Sift the flour and salt on to a work surface. Make a well in the center, add the butter and sugar, and gently work together with your fingertips. Add the yolks and gradually draw in the flour, adding drops of water as you go. When all the flour has been incorporated, form the dough into a ball, but do not overwork. Wrap in plastic wrap and refrigerate for at least 2 hours before use.

Crème anglaise

Makes 3⅔ cups

2 cups milk
1 vanilla bean, split
6 egg yolks
½ cup caster sugar

Bring the milk to a boil with the vanilla bean. Remove from the heat, cover, and let infuse for 10 minutes.

Beat the egg yolks with the sugar until thick and creamy. Bring the milk back to a boil and pour on to the yolk mixture, whisking continuously. Pour the mixture back into the saucepan and cook over low heat, stirring continuously with a spatula, until the custard thickens slightly.

Crème pâtissière

Makes 1¼ cups

3 egg yolks
¼ cup caster sugar
6 tablespoons all-purpose flour, sifted
1 cup milk

Whisk the yolks with the sugar until pale and creamy, then lightly whisk in the flour. Bring the milk to a boil and pour into the yolk mixture; stir to mix, then return to the saucepan and bring back to a boil, stirring continuously, for about 2 minutes. Remove from the heat and transfer to a bowl.

Crème Chantilly

¾ cup whipping cream, chilled
¼ cup confectioner's sugar
1 teaspoon vanilla extract
(optional)

Chantilly cream is served as an accompaniment to pastries, tarts, and other desserts.

Whisk the cream together with the sugar and vanilla until it forms soft peaks.

Index Page numbers in *italic* indicate illustrations.

Conversions

Liquid equivalents

METRIC	IMPERIAL	AMERICAN
15ml	1 tablespoon	
60ml	2fl oz	¼ cup
90ml	3fl oz	
100ml	3½ fl oz	
125ml	4fl oz	½ cup
150ml	5fl oz	⅔ cup
180ml	6fl oz	¾ cup
200ml	7fl oz	
250ml	8fl oz	1 cup
300ml	10fl oz (½ pint)	1¼ cups
375ml	12fl oz	1½ cups
500ml	15fl oz (¾ pint)	2 cups
600ml	1 pint	2½ cups
1 litre	1¾ pints	4 cups (1 quart)

Weight equivalents

METRIC	IMPERIAL	METRIC	IMPERIAL
15g	½oz	300g	10oz
20g	¾oz	325g	11oz
30g	1oz	350g	12oz
60g	2oz	375g	13oz
90g	3oz	400g	14oz
100g	3½oz	425g	15oz
120g	4oz	450g	1 lb
150g	5oz	500g	1 lb 2oz
175g	6oz	750g	1½lb
200g	7oz	900g	2lb
225g	8oz	1kg	2¼lb
250g	9oz	1.4kg	3lb

Oven temperatures

	°C	°F	gas
very cool	100–120	225–250	¼–½
	140	275	1
cool	150	300	2
warm	160	325	3
moderate	180	350	4
moderately hot	190	375	5
	200	400	6
hot	220	425	7
very hot	230	450	8
	240–250	475–500	9–10

Notes:

1 teaspoon = 5ml
1 tablespoon = 15ml
spoon measurements are level unless otherwise stated

pepper: use freshly ground black pepper unless otherwise stated

fresh ginger juice: grate a large piece (50–100g) of fresh ginger root into a small bowl, add 1–2 teaspoons dry white wine and leave for 1 hour. Pour the grated ginger and wine through a sieve into another bowl, pressing the ginger to extract all the flavour.

braising: all braised meat and poultry dishes improve with keeping, so make them the day before you want to serve them and leave to chill in their liquid; reheat just before serving.

turbot: I generally try to use large turbot of 8lb or more: the flesh will be firm, meaty and moist, and fish of this size is almost certainly wild, which is far superior to farmed fish.

lobsters: a whole lobster can be killed by plunging it into boiling water for 10–15 seconds. However, some recipes call for freshly killed lobster, and you should do this just before you begin the recipe. Make sure that the claws are secured with rubber bands, then place the lobster on a chopping board and hold its tail firmly, protecting your hand with a tea towel. Using a strong, very sharp, pointed knife, quickly and firmly pierce the lobster between the eyes – this kills it instantly.

With Very Best Wis

David Hemmi

and Hemmings

With Best Wishes

Dinner Party

SM Plaza

Copenhagen

SM Verdun

za Vernias

Merveilleuse Maîtour

pleine de charme et

d'intimité.

R Vaneur

Dany Chapel

... un délicieux repas

/ Christian Millau

une féerie gourmande 22/5/77

Georges Grade

Merci et Bravo —
grande cuisine —
S. Oger

P. Bocuse